DREAM OF
CONSCIOUSNESS

Contemplations on Advaita

Chaitanya S. Balsekar

Edited by
Gary Roba

YogiImpressions®

YogiImpressions®

DREAM OF CONSCIOUSNESS
First published in India in 2011 by
Yogi Impressions Books Pvt. Ltd.
1711, Centre 1, World Trade Centre,
Cuffe Parade, Mumbai 400 005, India.
Website: www.yogiimpressions.com

First Edition, April 2011

Copyright © 2011 by Chaitanya S. Balsekar

Cover concept and design by Shivdutt Sharma

ISBN 978-81-88479-76-4

Printed at: Repro India Ltd., Mumbai

Dedicated to
my Lord Shri Mangesh
with my love and gratitude
beyond measure.

Contents

FOREWORD

As a reader, I'm generally put off by long winded introductions, often passing them over in favor of the actual book. So, it's with some reticence that I'm following the impulse to write this and would thus certainly not blame you for just skipping over it and diving straight into this book. On the other hand, it's become good form for an editor to pen down some nonsense or the other, and as there does happen to be a story to be told here, if you're in the mood you may as well read on...

I met Chaitanya Balsekar about 9 or 10 years ago after one of his brother Ramesh's talks. I'd already been coming regularly to hear the talks for a few years at that point, but had somehow managed never to meet Chaitanya. Then one day he suddenly appeared out of nowhere as I was about to head out the door and down the stairs, introduced himself and invited me over to his apartment across the hall for some tea. Tea quickly turned into lunch, and 'hello my name is' turned equally quickly into an immediate and deep friendship. We've since continued our tea and lunch visits regularly several times a year whenever I found time to come to Bombay to hear Ramesh's daily talks.

Chaitanya and I naturally always enjoyed talking and sharing ideas about one of our favorite subjects, Advaita, and much of the time we spent together was occupied in this manner. It was not just the depth of his understanding that impressed me, but also the way in which he had so integrated both his guru Nisargadatta Maharaj's and his brother Ramesh Balsekar's teachings into it – a quality that's very present in this book. I was also always deeply moved and inspired by the way he so embodies Advaita in his daily life in the world.

One day, during one of our visits together, Chaitanya went into his study and came back with copies of some writings he'd recently jotted down, for me to read at my leisure. As soon as I read them I felt deeply touched by them, and each time I visited Bombay he was there waiting for me with a small stack of newer writings he'd done. I never expressed it to him but began on my own to secretly save up all of his writings into a small collection, because each time he gave them to me, beginning with that very first time, I was struck by an intense intuition that one day in the future after Ramesh had passed away I would find myself putting them together in the form of a book. I could quite literally 'see' it, like the preview of a film, and felt that it was my duty to follow through on it. There was never a doubt in my mind that this would eventually happen one day. I simply 'knew' it to be true.

The last time I saw Ramesh was about 5 months before he died. At that time he would often invite me to come visit with him in the afternoons privately, in addition to the public morning talks, and one such afternoon was the last time I was ever to see him. In what turned out to be our final conversation he asked me over a cup of tea why I had stayed around him all of these years, and what it was that he'd said when we first met that compelled me to keep returning. I replied that ever since my early childhood I continued to have the experience of 'seeing', 'knowing', or 'dreaming' things before they happened, often quite precisely, and sometimes well in the future... Getting suddenly very animated and cutting me off mid-sentence he completed the trail of my thought for me, nearly shouting, "Yes, yes Gary! Exactly! That is PROOF of it! The fact that some people see things or dream of things before they happen *proves* that the entire manifestation is already there in one big block! It is all already there! There is no denying it."

And then Ramesh – who had greatly alarmed me by the way he so spontaneously leapt out of his rocking chair while exclaiming this at full volume, toothless, like someone who'd just learned he'd won the lottery... after all he was 91+ years of age at this point, very frail, in poor health, and could barely get around even with the help of a walker – just as suddenly settled back down into his chair and into his normally passive but lucid witnessing type state, and returned to quietly sipping his tea again as if he were all alone in the room. After some time he very slowly hobbled over to the door with the help of the aforementioned walker to see me out, and the last thing he said before the door closed was, "So that's why you stayed for all these years. You knew from *personal experience* that it is true – no one does anything."

Well, it wasn't exactly the last thing he ever said to me from a certain point of view: 4 months later, on my way back to Bali where I was living at the time, from Brazil where I was visiting, I booked a flight with a stop-over in Bombay so I could go sit with Ramesh one last time and thank him deeply for everything he'd so selflessly given for all those years. I knew from my friend Gautam Sachdeva that Ramesh was dying, and I knew inside my heart that it was going to be my last ever chance to see him. Then, one week before the flight I had a dream; in the dream I was denied entry into India and was unable to see Ramesh or say goodbye to him. Waking up quite upset from this, I set myself to securing every possible document that Indian Immigration could conceivably ask for: my visa, hotel booking, onward flight ticket, bank statement, extra cash, etc., It seemed like overkill as I'd been to India more times than I can count and never had a problem, but I never the less gathered everything together into a folder in my carry on as I boarded the plane – interestingly, exactly one year ago this week.

Somewhere along the way I finally managed to fall asleep with my head pressed up against the side of the window, when I had another dream: I was back with Ramesh alone in his apartment and he told me, "Gary, I'm very sorry but they are not going to let you enter India this time. We won't be able to meet again." I got very upset and replied, "but Ramesh, this is my last chance to see you! I need to say goodbye and I need to thank you for everything you've given me. They *must* let me in!" Ramesh just laughed and said,

"This, like everything else, is destiny; it cannot be changed. But, it's also not important so don't be at all concerned with it. There's no need to say goodbye again. You've said goodbye to me so many times already and there's no need to thank me again either. You've already understood whatever I had to give you, and that understanding will take its natural course. There's no need for you to come back here anymore, so just be relaxed and smile as it happens." And, at that exact moment I was awoken from the dream by the plane's tires hitting down hard against the runway in Bombay.

In spite of the dream, I confidently approached the Immigration desk with my pre-prepared folder in hand, ready for any question the officer could throw at me. He immediately asked what country I'd flown in from and when I said, "Brazil," he replied, "Please show me the certificate for your yellow fever vaccine." After an oddly pregnant pause, I broke into a very enjoyable and hearty laughter. I'd never flown to Bombay from South America before and had no idea that one needed a vaccine for yellow fever to enter India from there! I couldn't stop laughing anymore than the officer could help having to deny me entry into the country. Ramesh passed away a few weeks later and although I felt deeply sad when I heard the news, I also couldn't help but smile as I knew that the story would have made Ramesh smile too.

So, when several months later Chaitanya sent me an email with an entire book length file of his most recent writings attached, informing me that he was considering compiling them into a book and asking if I'd be willing to edit the material for him, I again broke into a very deep and hearty laughter – having sat through the preview so many times before, I would finally be able to enjoy the actual film! As Ramesh pointed out so clearly on that final afternoon last spring, how is it that we can 'know' things before they happen unless those things are all already there? And, if they are all already there, then... 'game over'. I only stopped laughing once I downloaded the attachment and began reading through it – the material had exceptional depth and was very profoundly expressed. *Dream of Consciousness*, elucidates the fundamental tenets of Advaita as clearly and passionately as any book on the subject ever could. Even regardless of my previous premonitions about it, I felt compelled by the very words themselves to offer my assistance in any way possible to help get the book into print and immediately emailed Chaitanya to tell him so. I remain grateful that he took me up on the offer... though I know that he also couldn't help it.

By the way, speaking of Gautam Sachdeva – the publisher of this book: About 7 years ago while I was having a re-read of Ramesh's *Pointers from Nisargadatta Maharaj*, a clear voice came into my head and declared, "Someday someone will write a book called *Pointers from Ramesh Balsekar*." Naturally it was another one of those moments of uncontainable belly laughter when I received an email two years ago from Gautam expressing that he'd just written a book called, *Pointers from Ramesh Balsekar*, and asking if I'd mind proof reading it for him!

Have a look around you; though they are unique for each one of us, the signs are all so clearly there. How can one help but laugh? This entire manifestation so clearly *is* the *Dream of Consciousness*, and we are all both the Dreamer and the dreamed. However, it is up to each one of us to 'prove' this Truth for ourselves in the unique fires of personal experience, otherwise Advaita remains just a heap of strange sounding words.

And if somehow, in spite of the absurdity of it all, you still find yourself not laughing, somehow still not quite getting the joke, then please do read on... As you go through the following contemplations you'll likely notice things starting to look a bit different than they did before – less real and therefore more Real, less tangible and therefore far more Palpable. Get out of the way and let the contemplations do their work on you. With any luck, you may find yourself rolling around on the floor laughing hysterically, or perhaps on your knees expressing the deep gratitude that the cosmic punch-line inspires in one's heart. In fact, if somehow an obscure limited edition book like this has found its way into your hands and you're sitting there reading this right now, then that alone should be 'proof' enough that it was meant to be there. So go ahead, why not… turn the page and enjoy the deep journey through this beautiful book. After all, what have you got to lose? As Ramana Maharshi once said, "Your head is already in the tiger's mouth."

Or, as Chaitanya Balsekar might more soberly prefer to express it: May each one of us be lived to continually receive the deepest possible Understanding of the Truth about who and what we really are.

– Gary Roba,
Bangkok,
August 2nd 2010

PREFACE

This is a small book on Advaita but it is hard-core Advaita.*

No compromises.

I have tried to make Advaita as simple as possible, the way my own Understanding itself has evolved. You might agree with my Understanding or not. That is your privilege and your right. Nevertheless, Advaita beckons.

Advaita makes us aware of the invisibility that we are as Consciousness behind the visibility that we are as human beings. As human beings, we are but images temporarily appearing yet ultimately disappearing again, within the Pure Consciousness that we truly are beneath the mirage of our own manifestation. According to Advaita, Consciousness is all there is.

There is contemplation when the mind rests on a particular topic and becomes absorbed in it instead of flitting around aimlessly. This is a book of contemplations on Advaita. These contemplations are separate and independent of each other. Although you will find a lot of repetition in them, please consider each as if it is something entirely new that you are reading for the very first time. Read with sincerity, because there are always slight nuances to the apparently repetitious that contain 'something more'. They will make you increasingly grounded in the subject, because the point is not just to read *about* Advaita but to become grounded *in* Advaita. This is where the repetitions in the text come into the picture. Ultimately, Advaita will give us each our own personal understanding of it.

To get a good sense of the subject, you may initially read the whole book several times through if you so choose. After that, please read just one or two chapters a day with sincerity. In that way, let the book do its work insidiously. As you continue with the reading, you may find yourself understanding life without fearing it.

My brother Ramesh and I came to know of Nisargadatta Maharaj through an article by Jean Dunn in *The Mountain Path,* a periodical of Ramanashram. Fortunately, Maharaj used to stay nearby and we started attending the daily talks at his residence. Ramesh soon became one of the English translators for Maharaj's talks, which were given in Marathi. Maharaj was a very private person who firmly rejected any attempts to form an organization or institution around him. I was fortunate to be present when towards the end of his life Maharaj one day, just as privately, 'ordered' Ramesh to start giving his own talks. Other persons may also have been similarly 'ordered'. In any case, there was no question of any succession or successor. Ramesh's talks then started happening a few months after Maharaj passed away.

I remember once telling Maharaj that I could not understand a lot of what he was teaching. He said I should not worry about it because when he talked he planted seeds of Understanding, and they would take root in their own time. Truly enough, things have become far clearer to me to my own satisfaction.

I am also grateful to Ramesh for two vital clarifications:

The first is that the ego will remain so long as life is

there in the body. There is no such thing as killing the ego. The only difference between the ego of the Sage and that of an ordinary person is that the ego of the Sage has lost its sense of 'doership' and has become like a burnt rope, which appears but cannot bind.

The second is that life is a series of happenings for which no one is responsible.

This book came about after my friend Gautam Sachadeva read an article that I wrote on the Gayatri mantra. I had actually only written it for my own clarification and understanding, as well as for sharing with a few close friends, but after going through it Gautam inquired whether I was planning on writing a book. The fact that a publisher, who had also published my brother Ramesh's books among others, was asking me this question set me thinking, because prior to that writing a book had never been a possibility in my mind. However, it remained at that until another friend, Poonam Ahuja, did a numerological reading for me and said that I might be writing a book within the year! I want to sincerely thank these two friends for giving me the motivation to write this book – something that I had never dreamt of doing earlier but which has now happened.

Finally, I am extremely grateful to my friend Gary Roba for his brilliant editing, which has greatly enhanced the readability of this book. By 'cutting and polishing' this previously rough stone, Gary has made it sparkle like a diamond and masterfully brought in clarity wherever it was needed. Thank you Gary, I truly do appreciate it.

This is not a book for those who fear life, but for those who want to truly understand life and call its bluff!

May we all be lived to receive a deeper and deeper understanding of Advaita so that it plays an increasingly prominent role in our day to day living.

Now, please read on…

* Editor's note: It has become customary to compensate for the incapacity of the English language to accurately express Advaitic concepts that originated in Sanskrit by employing Capital and lower case letters for this purpose. Different authors have applied different strategies to this end, none of which are fully satisfying. Capitalizations generally represent the transpersonal or impersonal aspect of Consciousness, while lower case letters typically represent our personal everyday ego consciousness. In this book, we have endeavored to combine what seemed the best of these various, imperfect approaches in the hopes of not going too far wrong.

Throughout the text, I AM, and I AM THAT are fully capitalized when referring to either the pure Awareness of Being or to the Absolute, out of respect for the gravity that these terms have within contemporary Advaitic thought and literature. All other similarly oriented words, such as Consciousness, Awareness, Understanding etc., have simply had their first letter capitalized, except in specific instances where the author wished to emphasize their transcendent nature. Italics have been used wherever it was felt that specific emphasis would help clarify the meaning of a sentence. Although this approach seems to work for the most part, it is by nature still quite problematic. For example, writing "I AM THAT" would seem to create an object out of THAT, which in fact represents pure subjectivity. Furthermore, fully capitalizing THAT while only partially capitalizing Consciousness, Awareness, Being, etc., appears to create a hierarchy between THAT and Consciousness, when there clearly is none – they are exactly the same 'thing'. The deeper problem however has to do with the very expression of these concepts themselves, as to express the inexpressible truth of Advaita one is forced into the absurd position of linguistically objectifying the non-objectifiable nature of pure subjectivity, or of creating the mistaken impression that such theoretical subjectivity represents a permanent, separate individual – a ridiculous, conceptual game akin to building sandcastles without any sand!

If you are new to Advaita and find this to initially be rather confusing, don't be concerned. Simply keep reading and in time it will all start to make more sense. The same advice equally applies if you are not 'new' to Advaita yet the words still don't make much sense! Keep reading; stay with it. In fact, through the very attempt to understand the peculiar languaging of this philosophy, the meaning behind the words will begin to reveal itself to you. Find out, why is Consciousness capitalized on this page but not on the next? ['C' refers to Impersonal Consciousness and 'c' to personal consciousness]. Inquire, what causes the narrative to keep shifting unexpectedly between personal and impersonal perspectives? Keep exploring the material using your discrimination to ascertain why it has been written in the peculiar manner that it has. Find out in what way this odd means of writing in English helps to clarify the meaning of the concepts. The confusion one may initially feel when encountering these ideas for the first time [or the thousandth time] is actually a symptom of the concepts working on you! So, if you find yourself dazed and baffled, your mind drawing a complete blank after reading through a few pages, or perhaps even just a few lines, then congratulations – the teaching is working!!! However, fear not – in time, with any luck, it will all start appearing as simple as it truly is.

ADVAITA IN DAILY LIVING

The fundamental and basic concept of Advaita is that Consciousness, or God, or the Source is all there is. A-dvaita – not two. If that be so, then what is this manifestation and all of its innumerable contents, which include us? Where do they come in? In Advaita, it is Consciousness AS this manifestation, Consciousness AS me.

How can the philosophy of Advaita help me in my daily living?

Who is this me to be helped?

Here I am with this name and form, a human being with this human body, a human being with his hopes and desires, his ambitions and his wants, his joys and his pains, his victories and his failures, his anxieties and his frustrations. Here I am, a human being, facing life moment by moment, having to take decisions, having a certain position in life, and claiming such possessions as there are. I cannot get away from this human body, from this ego identified with this body, this ego with its free will and intellect, this ego with its sense of personal doership, and its sense of separation from others as well as from the Source. I cannot get away from the emotions and feelings that dominate and enslave me, and yet have become the 'raison d'être' of my life. As this ego who thinks he is this name and form, this human being, I have to live my life so long as there is life in this body.

How can Advaita help me in my day to day living? As Ramesh Balsekar often asked, "What use is any philosophy if it does not help us in our day to day living?"

Advaita first invites me to inquire into my real nature. What is my real nature? Who or what am I?

I identify with this body and call myself a human being, but am I actually this body? Of course, I am not this body. I AM THAT that is aware of this body as a vehicle for my journey through life from birth to death. I AM THAT that is aware of the acts that take place through this body according to its destiny.

I AM THAT that is aware of this body when it is in the waking state as my waking body. I AM THAT that is aware of the body in the dreaming state, which is my dream body. My dream world is as real to me in the dream state as my waking world is in the waking state. Furthermore, while in the deep sleep state I am not even aware of having a body at all. I am not even aware of myself. There are no waves. The water is still. However, this body is still living.

I am not these emotions, feelings, and thoughts, which affect the body. I AM THAT that is aware of them as they rise and set within me.

I am not this free will and intellect. I AM THAT that is aware of them as they are being used to produce the acts that take place through this body in its day to day life.

I am not this personality, this individual, or this ego, which conceives of itself as a human being. I AM THAT that is aware of the ego as it engages in the body's daily activities.

I AM THAT that is aware of the ego as it thinks it is the thinker of its thoughts, the doer of its acts, and the feeler of its feelings and emotions.

I AM THAT that is aware of the ego as it identifies with a position or an occupation in life.

I AM THAT that is aware of the ego as it identifies with various 'good' and 'bad' qualities e.g. I am loving, I am selfish, I am caring, I am angry.

I AM THAT that is aware of the ego as it identifies with various relationships in life e.g. I am a husband, I am a father, I am an enemy, I am a friend.

I AM THAT that is aware of the ego as it identifies with the so called achievements or failures that take place through the body according to its destiny (i.e. the body's destiny).

I AM THAT that is aware of the ego as it identifies with a particular name.

I AM THAT that is aware of the ego as it identifies with various 'personal' possessions.

Who am I then really? Who am I who is aware of all of these things yet remains independent of them? Who am I in my own right, not in relation to anyone or anything else?

I...AM. I EXIST. I AM Pure Existence: the Impersonal Awareness in which all of these things rise and set as thoughts, as movements of Consciousness, as ripples on the waters of my Being. Existence, Knowledge, Power, Peace... I AM. I do not have to think or believe that I exist. I KNOW I exist, prior to thought. That Knowledge, prior to thought, I AM. The moment I think or say "I AM," I have already moved out of KNOWLEDGE and into thought, the realm of the ego.

That Impersonal Awareness that, as Identified Consciousness, is aware as thought of this body, I AM. That that is aware as thought of the actions that take place through this body, I AM.

That Impersonal Awareness that, as Identified Consciousness, is aware of these emotions and feelings as thoughts, I AM.

That Impersonal Awareness that, as Identified Consciousness, is aware of this free will and intellect as thought, I AM.

That Impersonal Awareness that, as Identified Consciousness, is aware of the ego as thought, and of the ego's various activities as further thoughts, I AM.

I do not have to think "I AM." I do not have to believe "I AM." I know I AM, prior to thought.

I AM Impersonal Consciousness. As a human being I am an appearance of a human body within this manifestation, which itself is an appearance of Consciousness in Consciousness. I am, therefore, an appearance in Consciousness of Consciousness, and Consciousness is my content.

As a human being I am an illusion within Consciousness, with the further illusions of free will and intellect. Consciousness is the only reality. We are all just appearances of Consciousness in Consciousness, initially appearing then ultimately disappearing once again.

Just as different waves are nothing but movements of water within the water itself, we are all nothing but appearances of Consciousness within this Consciousness that is our very content. The waves are nothing but water, and we are nothing but Consciousness. And, just as the waves are being moved by the water, we are all being lived by Consciousness through the illusions of free will and intellect.

Ramesh Balsekar zeroed in on this point as the very essence of Advaita in day to day living: we do not live but are being lived by the Source.

With the application of this principle in our daily lives, we live with the Understanding: 'I am being lived to do this. I am being lived to think this. I am being lived to want this. I am being lived to feel this emotion'. Similarly, in the case of other people: 'They are being lived to do that. They are being lived to think that. They are being lived to want that. They are being lived to feel that emotion'. In short, whatever we think, or feel, or want, or do is exactly what we are supposed to do and we cannot act in any other way.

When we totally believe that we are all part of the same Source, and that we are all mutually being lived by that one Source, what happens? Judgment of ourselves and of others flies out the window and we are free from its burden – free from its resentments, its condemnations, its hatreds, its arrogance, its fears, its regrets, its envies, its jealousies, and so on. We accept life as it happens. And, there is no separation between ourselves and others within the one Consciousness that we all are. Consciousness is all, as all.

My Self Image is of Consciousness appearing as a human

being within Consciousness itself. I now know that I do not live but am being lived by Consciousness. Therefore, as a human being, I now know that I am but a role being played by the one true Actor, Consciousness. As far as my day to day living is concerned, I think, and feel, and act as if I have total freedom. However, at the very same time, I know that whatever I think, or feel, or do is exactly what I am supposed to think, or feel, or do as a role according to the Divine Script. The consequences that I experience as a result of what I think, or feel, or do are also exactly what I am supposed to experience as a role according to my destiny. If I happen to receive those consequences with acceptance, joy, resentment, or resistance, or in any other manner, that is equally exactly how I am meant to receive them.

With this Understanding, there is total acceptance of life exactly as it is with no 'ifs', 'buts', or 'if onlys'. If a cold breeze disturbs us, we do not condemn the wind and blame it for blowing. We simply protect ourselves by wearing some warm clothing. Similarly, if we have been cheated a couple of times by a person, what is the sense in sitting in judgment over him blaming him for 'his' supposed actions? We simply take care to protect our future interests to whatever extent possible. There is wisdom in discernment, but only ignorance in condemnation.

The initial intellectual understanding of Advaita has to deepen and deepen until, either suddenly or gradually, it becomes a true and total Understanding. It can only happen and can never be made to happen. Of course, we will try to make it happen if it says so in our script but it can only actually happen if it also says so in the script. We cannot hasten the dawn by waking up early. However, we may be lived to wake up early if we are to see the dawn.

Having seen the one true sun rise for the first time with our very own eyes, with the light of Consciousness shining upon us, we will finally be enabled to see clearly and to fully accept ourselves as we are with no guilt or self contempt for our mistakes and failures, and no arrogance or pride for our victories and achievements. Equally, there will be no resentment, hatred, or envy against others because it is clear that they are also being lived by Consciousness. As our compulsion to live in judgment over the world becomes less and less, we will feel as if a tremendous load is being lifted from our shoulders. We will start feeling light and free. We will start taking note of the facts and events as they arise, without adding on our emotional interpretations. Absent our need to identify with them, they will remain exactly what they are – just facts and events. We will be lived to simply witness life without judgment distorting our view.

And, we will be blessed with freedom from the tyranny and fear of our emotions and feelings. We will no longer be afraid of them, no matter what they are.

In the daily flow of life all things simply come, remain, and then go, but we do not identify with them. We allow them to be the pointers to the Consciousness that is the content of the thoughts that they are. Through our acceptance of and non-reactivity to them, they become our benefactors. We take our stand in Consciousness and let life flow.

PRAYER

When our attention is directed towards God, no matter what the reason, it is prayer.

Therefore, it is prayer even when we are just asking God for something that we want, because our attention is thereby directed towards God – our Source.

However, prayer becomes deeper and deeper as we become more and more consciously aware with gratitude of our oneness with God at all times, in all circumstances.

Without a doubt, our capacity for awareness is one of the most valuable things in life, because life is lived where our awareness is.

There cannot be a greater use of our awareness than when it is directed inwards to the Impersonal Consciousness that we are.

Our whole life becomes a prayer when our awareness is continually directed spontaneously to whatever we happen to be doing, with the understanding that we are being lived by the Source to do it because we and the Source are one.

Our whole life becomes a prayer when we experience everything no matter what, with the understanding that we are being lived to experience it by the Source because we and the Source are one.

Whenever we think of God, or the Source, or Consciousness, may we be lived to do so with gratitude and love because we are being given the opportunity by God to be aware of Him.

As one philosopher has so wisely said:
See you with love all things that you see,
Soon you will see all things that you love.

Do I, the ego, look out and see only the bars of this body, or do I reach out to the stars with love and lose myself in the Infinite Here and the Eternal Now?

Blessed is the day when we look at the things of this world and know with absolute clarity that we are looking at appearances of Consciousness in Consciousness, and that Consciousness is their very content!

Blessed is the day when we look at other human beings and see with unwavering clarity that they are but appearances of Consciousness in Consciousness, and Consciousness is their very content!

Blessed is the day when we look upon ourselves and see with stainless awareness that we are but appearances of Consciousness in Consciousness, and that Consciousness is our very content!

Blessed is the day when we look upon all things and only see God – Consciousness – Source – Self.

Thy Will be done.

THE UNDERSTANDING

Before I try to investigate the nature of this manifestation of which I am but a part, let me first contemplate upon my own nature.

Who or what am I? I am Chaitanya Balsekar. This is only a name, which is used to identify me. It can be changed to any other name. Therefore, obviously, I am not this name.

Who or what am I? I call myself a human being because I identify with this human body. However, this human body is only a vehicle that carries me through the journey of life from its birth to its death. I cannot be my body because I AM THAT that is aware of it as my vehicle.

Who or what am I? I am these emotions, feelings, and thoughts, which I experience all the time that I'm awake or dreaming and with which I identify. I experience and identify with each emotion, feeling, or thought as it appears and disappears. However, they come and go while I remain. Therefore, I am not these emotions, feelings, and thoughts. I AM THAT that is aware of them.

Who or what am I? I am this free will and intellect that enable me to judge, think, and act. However, I can't really be either this free will or this intellect because I AM THAT that is aware of them. Therefore, they must just be my tools.

Who or what am I? I am this me, this ego, this individual, this personality that is separate from other individuals or egos, who is the doer of his deeds, the thinker of his thoughts, and the experiencer of his emotions and feelings. However, when I consider this me or ego, I realize that this me is really only notional and totally owes its existence to this body. Where is this me, this ego who considers itself to be an individual separate from other individuals, unless this body and the other bodies are taken into account?

Where is this me or ego who has emotions, feelings, and thoughts, without the body also coming into the picture?

Where is this me or ego who can decide to do something and has the free will to do it, unless the body is also taken into account? Where is this me or ego who is a husband, son, brother, or friend to other individuals, without also taking the body into account? Where is this me or ego who holds a certain position in life or has certain possessions, without also taking the body into account?

Therefore, it is clear that this ego must go together with this body, and this me or ego is only notional as it cannot exist without the body.

As expressed earlier, this body is only a vehicle that from its birth to its death carries me through the journey of life. I am not this vehicle but THAT that is aware of it. Similarly, I am not this me or ego that goes along with the body through the journey of life. I AM THAT that is aware of it.

Then who am I who is aware of this body, these thoughts, these feelings and emotions, this will and intellect, this me or ego? Who am I in my own right, not dependent upon any of these external perceptions? The only answer can be I AM. Not I am this or that, but I AM. Pure Impersonal Presence, Impersonal Awareness, or Consciousness I AM in which all of these other apparent subjects rise and set as thought-objects.

Just as the water is the source of the waves that rise and set within it and is also the very content of the waves, this I AM – or Impersonal Awareness as Presence – is the source of all of the thoughts that rise and set within it and is their very content as Identified Consciousness.

The answers that I come to can only be in thought. And, while thought can be a pointer to the Truth it can never actually be the Truth. Truth can never be understood. It can only be experienced, and when it is experienced there is no ego present to experience it. Thus, you cannot experience Truth. You can only be Truth.

When Consciousness is still and at rest, such as in deep sleep or while unconscious, it is not even aware of itself. Therefore, it is only when there are thoughts or movements in Consciousness that there is awareness of this ego, this body, and this manifestation. In the space between two thoughts, or when there are no thoughts or movements in Consciousness, then the ego and the manifestation disappear once again. Or, in such a case as the meditative state of Turiya, which is also absent of ego, body, manifestation, thoughts or movements in Consciousness, there is only Pure Awareness: Consciousness, aware only of itself.

Ultimately, this is what I AM, Silent Witnessing Presence. Yes, Silent Witnessing Presence in the waking and dreaming states, Silent Witnessing Presence of the absence of Presence in the deep sleep state, and Silent Witnessing Presence of Presence in the thought free state, which is my original nature.

What then do I make of this individual, this personality or ego, this body, these emotions and feelings, this intellect and will, along with all of the other people and objects in the manifestation?

How is Impersonal Awareness connected with this particular human being, this particular body/mind, and this vast manifestation?

What is the human being, and what is this manifestation?

This manifestation that is the waking world of each one of us is nothing other than the Dream of Consciousness, in a manner of speaking. In this manifestation, wherever bodies appear Consciousness gets identified with them as the life within those bodies, i.e. 'Identified Consciousness'. A human being appears as a body/mind unit. Accordingly, the thought movements within this body/mind unit, or Identified

Consciousness, create the appropriate ego for this human being in its waking world manifestation.

When I fall asleep and dream, I create my own dream world in which I have a dream body and a dream ego, along with all of the other dream egos, dream persons, and dream objects. In this dream, my dream world is as real to my dream ego as this waking world is to my waking ego when I am awake. Upon waking up, the dream world vanishes into Consciousness and the waking world takes its place. However, if instead of waking up I fall into deep sleep, the dream world that arose in Consciousness will disappear again, back into Consciousness. There, there are no thoughts because Consciousness is still and at rest, unaware even of itself.

When I wake up, for the first few miniscule moments in most cases, there is Pure Awareness without thought – Silent Witnessing Presence of Presence – I AM. Then, movement spontaneously stirs within Consciousness and thoughts arise in this body/mind unit along with the ego, the body, and the waking world manifestation. The waking state has now taken over.

Every thought that arises in this human being must have

its two ends, just as there cannot be a stick without two ends. The two ends of a thought are the subject end and the object end. The subject end is always the ego or personality connected with the body, while the object end may be whatever it is in each case depending upon the nature of the thought. Therefore it is a thought, or movement in Identified Consciousness, that creates the ego identified with the body. The ego is a creation of the thought, and not the creator of the thought. Identified Consciousness and the ego are essentially the same thing because Identified Consciousness is the content of the ego.

But then, how does Identified Consciousness become aware of the manifestation? Identified Consciousness becomes aware of the manifestation through the senses of each body/mind unit in which it gets reflected or identified, or through the object in which it is reflected or identified. Therefore, the 'reality' of the manifestation will be different for each body/mind, or each object, according to the nature of the body or object. The reality of the manifestation for a man born blind, or a man born deaf and dumb, will obviously be very different from that of a man born with those senses. It will also naturally be quite different for different human beings in general, and very, very different for a stone or an insect.

How then does Consciousness becomes aware of the manifestation through the senses? When light from an object strikes the eye there is an impulse that goes to the brain and there is a thought, "I am seeing this object." This is the SEEING thought. The subject end is the ego 'I', and the object end is the relevant object that is being seen.

Similarly, there is the HEARING thought:
I am hearing this sound. I'm hearing you talk.

Similarly, there is the SMELLING thought:
I am smelling wonderful food. I'm smelling this awful stink.

Similarly, there is the TOUCHING thought:
I am touching this soft cloth. I'm feeling this soft skin.

Similarly, there is the TASTING thought:
I'm finding this food very tasty.

There can also be thoughts apart from the senses such as those in the realm of pure concepts:

I am thinking that freedom is my birthright. I'm thinking that this cloth gives better value for money than the other one.

Then there are other types of thoughts like WILLING thoughts and DOING thoughts:

I will do this. I will not do that. I will take a decision later. I am doing this act. I am the doer of this act, etc.

And, then there are also memory thoughts:
I remember my friend from school.

By now it will be clear that all thoughts rising and setting within a human body/mind, or Identified Consciousness, create an appropriate ego as the subject end of each thought, the object end depending upon the nature of the object concerned. It will also be clear that the so called reality of the manifestation cannot be the same for all body/mind units or objects.

To repeat: when I am dreaming, an entire dream world is created in my dream. That dream appears within this body/mind. The dream world appears as real to the dreamed me, or dream-ego, as this waking world appears to the awake me, or waking-ego. Upon awakening, the dream world including the dream ego disappears back into Identified Consciousness. Similarly, this manifestation is the dreamed world of Impersonal Consciousness, and we are all dreamed egos of that Consciousness. Consciousness is the Dreamer, the one Actor playing all the roles of the different egos and objects in this dream. However, the dream egos in this Dream of Consciousness do not realize that they are just roles being played by the one true Actor. They believe that this dream world, or manifestation, is real and that they are also real, while the Actor – Consciousness or the Dreamer – is illusory.

Sri Nisargadatta Maharaj described this manifestation as a movie or drama written by Consciousness, directed and produced by Consciousness, with all of the roles being acted by Consciousness, and with the audience also being nothing but Consciousness! Therefore, in this Divine Movie, we are all just roles played by Consciousness. Each role will be played until there is no life left in that particular body appearance. When 'life' ends, the role will end. My role will end when this body dies, and this ego and Identified Consciousness will end with it.

Through Divine Hypnosis, or Maya, the roles in this Divine Movie believe that they are real, while Consciousness the Actor is thought to be illusory. However, in a few roles there is what may be called Self-realization, when it is realized that as roles we are all illusions while as Consciousness the Actor we are Reality. Even then those roles still continue to be played as long as there is life in their bodies, but now with the Understanding that as roles they do not live but are being lived by the Actor, according to His script, along with all of the other roles. Consciousness is all, as all. Consciousness is all there is.

But, what about all of our unfulfilled desires, dreams and aspirations, the talents which we have acquired, our good deeds, our sins? What happens to them? The notional ego that was identified with the body will end with the body. However, one's unfulfilled desires, dreams and aspirations, one's talents, good deeds, sins, and so on will not be wasted; they will join the pool of Consciousness. When new bodies appear within the manifestation, parts from the pool will be attached to the different bodies according to whatever proportions the destiny of those new bodies requires.

The question then arises: If this is indeed the case then why should I bother to do good deeds, to help others, to do my duty, and so on if I do not benefit thereby in 'my' next life? I might as well live as selfishly, as meanly, and as cruelly as I want. This question reveals that I have still not accepted the concept that I am not the doer, the understanding that I do not live but am being lived. I therefore still believe that

I am the doer of my actions, that I live my life, and that my life is not being lived for me. If I had fully accepted the concept of non-doership then such a question could not have arisen, because there would be no question of my deciding how to live. The concept is that just as I am being lived to act in certain ways in the course of my life, so also will I be lived to face the consequences such as they may be, according to the Divine Script, in this very life.

How then do I live my life? Do I live in a state of psychological paralysis, disconnected from the free will I am meant to have? No. Having accepted this concept totally, first and foremost I accept the here and now of life without any resentment or resistance. I live fully, using my apparent free will with the understanding that whatever I think or do, I would not think or do unless I was being lived in exactly that way. I understand that just as I am being lived as I am, other people are also being lived as they are whether they are aware of it or not. I therefore do not sit in judgment over them while calculating a response to 'their' actions.

It is this aspect of the ego, namely the non-doership of the ego that Ramesh focused on. When the ego ponders over the actions of the day that the ego feels certain were its own actions, it soon realizes that they were all preceded by a specific thought that triggered them. The arising of that particular thought, at that exact moment in time, was something over which the ego obviously had no control whatsoever. Upon seeing the truth of this with clarity, the ego cannot help but accept that any action arising in response to a thought it had no control over cannot possibly be the direct action of the ego. Through repeatedly awakening to this fact, the ego must inevitably come to the conclusion that it was never the doer! It could never have been the doer; it was always just an illusory role, never the one true Actor that Consciousness always is.

To repeat: as long as there is life in the body, the reflected I AM, as Identified Consciousness, gets identified with that body and its name in the form of an ego, a role that is then played by Consciousness. Thus far, it is neutral and harmless. It is only when the ego assumes that it truly has free will, choice, and doership, it is only when the role begins to believe that it is the Actor that the whole mischief begins. As Ramesh pointed out, the ego as identification with the body and its name cannot be eliminated as long as there is life in that body. Only when Understanding takes place and the ego's mischievous sense of doership – that cause of all of its fear, sorrow, and frustration – gets eliminated, or neutralized, does the ego live in acceptance and peace, free from its imagined separation from the Source.

All that has been considered above are nothing more than concepts, which some people will accept and others will reject. They will continue to remain as mere concepts until Understanding or Self-realization sets in. To each his own concepts, to each his own path! Meanwhile, the only Truth for us in phenomenality is I AM, that Impersonal Presence, that Impersonal Awareness or Consciousness prior to thought that we all are, and which none of us can deny. Even a person who has amnesia, while he may run around asking who he is, will not question his own being, I AM, which is prior to thought. This is our proof, our evidence, of the Divine Consciousness that we all are.

To conclude: I live with the total Understanding that I live, breathe, move, and have my being in Consciousness, that Consciousness and I are one, and that Consciousness is all there is. As I continue to live the Understanding, more and more does my attention get directed to the Consciousness that I AM, and more and more to the Peace that Consciousness is.

Gradually, the heavy load of judging everything, including the judging of myself and others, gets lighter and lighter as the judging gets less and less.

More and more does the immediate acceptance of 'what is' occur.

More and more does my attention get directed to what I have, and less and less to what I do not have.

More and more does my attention get directed to what I AM, and less and less to what I only appear to be.

More and more, gratitude arises… and remains.

IMPERSONAL CONSCIOUSNESS, IDENTIFIED CONSCIOUSNESS AND THE EGO

I.

When Impersonal Consciousness, not yet even aware of itself, suddenly becomes aware that it 'exists' it also simultaneously appears as the manifestation. The manifestation is an appearance of Consciousness in Consciousness. It literally appears – to exist.

As parts of the manifestation, all objects and beings are also appearances of Consciousness in Consciousness. Impersonal Consciousness identifies with each one of them translating into Identified Consciousness.

Every Identified Consciousness relates to Impersonal Consciousness in exactly the same way as every image of the sun, in different ponds of water, reflects the same one true sun in the sky.

Within human beings, Identified Consciousness becomes subject to the various states of the organism – the deep sleep state, the waking state, and the dreaming state.

Although Impersonal Consciousness, identified with a human body as Identified Consciousness, remains pure within thought-free states such as deep sleep and Samadhi, the usually continuous run of thoughts in the waking and dreaming states creates the ego as the subject end of every arising thought.

Identified Consciousness gets identified thereby with both the body *and* the ego, as the subject of all other objects.

II.

When Impersonal Consciousness, not yet even aware of itself, suddenly becomes aware that it exists it simultaneously becomes identified with the manifestation as I AM. In other words Impersonal Consciousness, identified or reflected in the various objects within the manifestation, becomes Identified Consciousness. Therefore, there's really no difference between Impersonal Consciousness and Identified Consciousness. They are exactly the same.

It is only when thought arises in Identified Consciousness that Identified Consciousness appears as the ego; until then, there is no ego. Although unaware of itself, Identified Consciousness continues in deep sleep because it still remains identified with the body, which is alive and breathing.

Again, Identified Consciousness only becomes the ego with the arising of thoughts within itself. Except for brief periods in deep sleep and in the momentary gap between thoughts, Identified Consciousness is subject to a nearly continuous barrage of thoughts. Therefore, as far as we human beings are concerned, Identified Consciousness is as good as the ego.

While still living, the highest state one can reach is the thought-free state of Pure Identified Consciousness, i.e. Impersonal Consciousness reflected in the body as Identified Consciousness prior to the arising of the ego. However, this can only be a passing state because the ego immediately resumes with the arising of thoughts.

The reflection of Impersonal Consciousness as Identified Consciousness only ceases with the death of the body. This is ultimately only notional of course because it was always Impersonal Consciousness the whole time.

III.

To conclude:

I AM is Pure Identified Consciousness, the Presence prior to thought behind the body appearance. It is the identification of Impersonal Consciousness within the manifestation with the awareness that it exists.

When thought or movement stirs within it, Identified Consciousness – I AM – becomes 'I am xyz' with whom it becomes identified as the ego.

ADVAITA AND DVAITA

Advaita and Dvaita are the two main streams of Indian Philosophy. Though the two are quite separate and distinct, they are generally intermingled in everyday Indian thought unknowingly. We mix concepts from Advaita and Dvaita all the time without realizing it, thereby creating a lot of confusion.

Dvaita means 'two', referring to duality; A-dvaita means 'not two', or "non-duality." The fundamental difference between them is one of self image.

In Dvaita, the self image of a human being is that of a soul passing from birth to birth, carrying its baggage of karmic merits and de-merits, consecutively acquiring new bodies until at long last it becomes so pure and perfected that it merges into God, or Pure Consciousness.

In Advaita, the Self image of a human being is that he is an appearance of Consciousness in Consciousness itself, meaning he is already nothing but Consciousness right here and now. All that happens upon the death of the body appearance is that Impersonal Consciousness ceases to appear as Identified Consciousness, identified with that body appearance as an ego.

In Advaita, the human being is like a wave appearing within and being lived by the water that is its very content. Each wave, which is totally powerless in-and-of itself, is being moved by the power of the water as an expression of the integrated movement of the entire ocean, and we could thus call each *apparently separate* wave's movements – such as how big or long it will be, how strongly it will swell, how long it will last, etc. – that wave's 'destiny'.

In Dvaita, each wave is believed to have the personal power to determine its own destiny with its free will. Thus, each individual human ego is to be held accountable for *its* actions and must reap the consequences of those actions, whether 'good' or 'bad', from birth to birth. Whereas in Advaita, the ego with its ostensible free will is only a mechanism through which the presumed individual is being lived by Consciousness, and that ego will therefore die along with the body. There can be no question of a mechanism's 'rebirth'. An appearance of a human being has manifested in Consciousness, and upon its 'death' will disappear again back into Consciousness. That is it.

It is up to each of us to inquire: do I believe that the wave lives its own separate and independent life, creating its own reality through its individual intentions and personal power, or do I believe the wave to be lived, moved, and 'breathed' solely by the power of the water according its destiny?

Is my self image that of a soul passing from birth to birth, or is my Self image that of Consciousness itself? One's answers reveal their particular allegiance to the streams of Dvaita or Advaita. For many, the answers may seem blurry due to the general confusion that exists about this subject.

A common misunderstanding of Advaita is when a person thinks that he will become like a vegetable by accepting this concept; he will not want to do anything and will just lie around. But on the contrary, if one accepts this concept totally he will continue to be lived according to his destiny, just as he's always been. One may equally ask, "If I am powerless to *do* anything, then how will I live my life?" But, if one is being lived by Consciousness then where is the question of taking a decision about how to live one's life?

Another common misunderstanding gives rise to the objection, "But surely there are consequences to my actions, and society will still hold me responsible for what I have *done!*" Yes, this is true, but Advaita points out that just as I am being lived by Consciousness, I am also being lived to experience the consequences of my so being lived.

It must be remembered that as a follower of Advaita I will have just as many goals and will put in just as much effort to achieve them as a follower of Dvaita will do. The only vital difference is that because I am aware that I am being lived to do so, I equally know that the results of my efforts are not in my hands and will thus be exactly as they are supposed to be. Therefore, why worry over the results or consequences of *my* actions?

Whether we subscribe to Dvaita or Advaita will obviously also be in conformance with the way we are being lived according to our destiny.

To conclude: In Dvaita, one is a soul that is striving to evolve and merge into Impersonal Consciousness, i.e.

"to become one with God."

In Advaita, it is recognized that we already are one with God as we are all nothing other than Impersonal Consciousness, appearing temporarily as Identified Consciousness until life 'departs' from the body. There can therefore be no question of *achieving* any so-called 'spiritual evolution'.

In Advaita, we transcend our allegiance to the petty mind with its incessant need to explain life by determining and judging what is right, good, logical, or just.

With this Understanding, one completely accepts and knows – I AM Totality…

And, Consciousness, or Totality, is all there is.

THERE ARE NOT TWO POWERS

We are used to judging things as good or evil, beautiful or ugly, attractive or repulsive, etc. In so doing, we are conferring upon appearances the power of 'good and evil', and thereby judging all events as either good happenings or bad happenings.

What we must realize instead is that Consciousness is the only power, and that all of these appearances have no power of their own beyond that which we imagine them to have. They are truly only appearances.

When a so called evil deed is perceived to have been done, all that has actually happened is that we've had a thought: "I am seeing this terrorist killing so many people." Believing the event to have independent existence and the personal power implied in that, we judge both the deed and the perpetrator of that deed, the terrorist, as 'evil'.

We, as 'I – the ego', are the subject end of that thought, while the object end is the 'evil' deed. The perceiver and the perceived are but two ends of a thought, the content of which is nothing but Consciousness. Therefore, Consciousness is both the ego *and* the so called 'evil' deed. The deed has no power of its own, whether of good or evil. It is only an appearance within the one true power – Consciousness.

May we always be aware that all external events are actually just happenings in Consciousness, and Consciousness is their only content. They are just appearances, and as such, there is no inherent power in them.

Our perception of events may lead us to feel happy or sad, peaceful or agitated, etc., but while we are experiencing them let us remain aware that they are truly nothing but Consciousness.

THE BODY IS THE FOOD
OF IDENTIFIED CONSCIOUSNESS

When the I AM gets reflected in or identified with a body appearance within the manifestation, Impersonal Consciousness becomes Identified Consciousness identified with that body appearance.

The body thus becomes 'the food' that that Identified Consciousness sustains itself on, for as long as the body continues to live.

When the body dies, Impersonal Consciousness ceases to appear as that Identified Consciousness or that ego, since Identified Consciousness obviously cannot survive without its food, the living body.

Concerning the subject of our survival after death as spirits: When our bodies die, our appearance as egos disappears along with the appearance of life in our bodies. The Identified

Consciousness dissolves back into the Impersonal Consciousness it was always just a reflection of.

Although those who survive us may believe we are still in contact with them as spirits, this belief can only appear in the form of a thought, feeling, sense, or dream – the contents of which are nothing but Consciousness.

Consciousness has appeared as us, and Consciousness has ceased to appear as us.

That is it, as far as Advaita is concerned.

WE ARE ALL THE ONE CONSCIOUSNESS

I am here as a human being because there is life in this human body. If there were no life in this body, I would only be a human corpse.

What is this 'life'? It is Consciousness.

It is only due to Consciousness that I am aware of myself at all, or aware of you and the rest of this manifest world of which we are all a part.

When I see you, the light that is reflected off of your body strikes my eyes, and there is a thought in Consciousness that 'I am seeing you'. If there were no Consciousness, even if my eyes were wide open, there would be no thought and therefore no question of my seeing you.

When I am aware of myself, the light of Consciousness

strikes my body and is reflected within it as the awareness that I AM. In the absence of Consciousness there would be no question of any awareness of my being.

When I am aware of you, when I see you and talk to you, it is only because this Consciousness is there within me. This same principle equally applies to my hearing you, my touching you, my smelling you, my feeling you, etc.

You, 'me', and the rest of this world are nothing but thoughts, movements, or vibrations in this Consciousness that I AM.

I am not the body that constitutes this human corpse but the Consciousness that constitutes this human being. You, 'me', and the rest of this apparent world are nothing but thoughts within MY Consciousness.

Because you can also say exactly the same thing about me, 'you', and this world, the Consciousness I AM as a human being must be the same Consciousness YOU ARE as a human being, and a tree IS as a tree, etc.

Consciousness is Spirit. It has no limitations and is infinite.

Spirit only appears to be limited when it identifies itself with a body as the 'life' within that body. When Spirit as the life of the body leaves that body, the Identified Consciousness is reabsorbed into the Impersonal, Infinite Consciousness it was always just a reflection of.

We *are* the same Consciousness that is the content of all the different 'lives' of the different bodies appearing within it, just as the same water is the content of the different waves appearing within the ocean, which all waves are yet another movement within.

We are human body appearances, appearances of Consciousness in Consciousness, and Consciousness is our content. We are all the one Consciousness just as the waves are all the one water.

When I look at you, I look at you with the Understanding that YOU ARE what I AM, for we are all truly nothing but the one Consciousness in which we are all appearing.

We *are* Spirit.

THOUGHTS

All the so-called events that we see are ultimately nothing but thoughts.

I am seeing this horrible event happening.

I am seeing this wonderful event happening.

I am enjoying this wonderful occasion.

These are all thoughts in Consciousness and Consciousness is their content. Consciousness is all there is. There is no special power for good or evil in the event, although we may believe it to be so. Consciousness is the only power behind all events. Consciousness is the only power.

What happens if we see a man being murdered by another

person? This is actually a thought in our minds that we are seeing this event happening. Consciousness is the content of this thought. How do we react to the event? We are also appearances of Consciousness in Consciousness, and Consciousness is also our content. Therefore, we will react exactly as we are lived by Consciousness to react.

We might be lived to rush to the man's rescue. We might be lived to shout fiercely calling for help or to stand there paralyzed, or to run away.

Whatever happens, that is the way we are being lived by Consciousness in Consciousness. If we are being lived to run away from the happening and then to curse ourselves as cowards, then that is exactly the way we are meant to be lived. If we rush to help the person and get hurt in the process, then that is exactly the way we are meant to be lived, although others may then be lived to call us foolhardy.

This human being that we think we are is being lived in two ways: the body is being lived breath by breath, and the mind is being lived thought by thought.

Thoughts arise in Identified Consciousness and create the ego as their subject end, while their object end depends upon the nature of the particular thought.

Thoughts arise in Identified Consciousness, which is basically nothing but Impersonal Consciousness identified with a body appearance appearing within itself. Therefore, the content of *all* of the thoughts that are continually arising within Identified Consciousness is truly nothing but Impersonal Consciousness.

Consciousness is all there is.

Therefore, whenever we pause to consider that the thoughts we are presently thinking, no matter how sublime, or dirty, or mundane they may be, are nothing but Consciousness – which is their very content – we immediately recognize that we are always one with Consciousness throughout the day.

We are thus in meditation all of the time in the midst of all our daily activities.

THE EGO IS A THOUGHT
IN PRESENCE

The ego is a thought. How can a thought think another thought or perform an action?

'I am doing this act', is not the ego actually *performing* an action but a thought rising and setting in Consciousness. An action is happening. 'I am doing this action', is a thought concerned with that action, a subject-thought concerned with that object-action.

'I am feeling angry', is not really the ego *feeling* angry. It is another thought in its own right, rising and setting in Consciousness. The feeling of anger is there. 'I am feeling angry', is a thought concerned with that feeling, a subject-thought concerned with that object-feeling.

'You have done this act to hurt me', is likewise nothing more than a thought. It is an accusation-thought concerned with an action that has apparently 'happened', within which a subject-thought (me) gets created by organizing around an object-thought (you).

These are all just thoughts rising and setting within Consciousness, including the ego-thought 'me'.

But what I really am, prior to thought, is the Impersonal Consciousness that is identified with this body appearance as Identified Consciousness.

The ego is merely a thought concerned with the Identified Consciousness or Presence that I AM, and my Presence is thus the very content of that ego-thought, as well as of all of the other thoughts that arise within ME.

The ego is truly only a creation of thought, and is not the creator of thought. And all thoughts, including the ego, can only arise within Presence.

May my attention rest in the Presence I AM, and not on me the ego that gets created by the various thoughts continually rising and setting within ME.

All thoughts rise and set within my Presence. They come

and go while I remain.

I remain, prior to thought, as the screen on which the movie of life is projected by my Self, within my Self, and as my very Self.

GOD'S WILL

Everybody *talks* about "not a thing happening, not a leaf moving, unless it is the will of God." However, to my mind, Ramesh was one of the very, very few who gave this all the importance that it deserved, and more. As far as he was concerned this is a vital aspect of Advaita, because Ramesh always believed that any philosophy worth the name was of no use unless it helped one in one's daily living. He taught that the concept of God's will, or the impersonal functioning of totality, prevailing everywhere all the time is the key factor to live by in day to day life.

It helps one in so many remarkable ways. The foremost is that it keeps one connected with the Source all the time. When one lives with the realization that whatever one does is exactly what one is supposed to do according to the will of God, then what better way can there be than this to remain connected with the Source in daily living?

On the other hand, when one thinks that one acts of one's own free will and intellect then this instantly separates one from the Source. There is instant separation. Then whatever one does in life, whatever success and prosperity one achieves or does not achieve, one always wants more. There is always something lacking. One is never happy or fulfilled. There's always pain – one may not realize it but this pain is the pain of separation from the Source, which is the price of the free will that one believes in.

The second remarkable thing is that it frees one from the curse of judgment: judgment of ourselves, of others, and of life itself. When we realize that we do not live but are being lived by Consciousness as appearances of Consciousness in Consciousness, then where is the question of sitting in judgment over ourselves or others?

Life is a procession of happenings of which we are a part but not the cause. We accept life as it is, as it unfolds, but first we accept it. We use our so called free will and intellect but do so knowing that whatever we think, or feel, or want, or do is precisely what we are being lived to think, or feel, or want, or do.

We accept life. We flow with it, staying connected with

the Source all the time. We may desire a change and may even try to bring about a change in ourselves or our circumstances if we are lived to do so, but we accept whatever actually happens.

The ego is the mechanism through which Consciousness functions within living beings, and through which life is lived by them. Therefore, as Ramesh maintained, there can be no question of killing the ego. The ego must remain so long as life and thoughts continue. The question is only of understanding the ego. The ego of the average person believes that it 'has' free will and intellect, and is thus accountable for 'its' actions. The ego of the sage also lives with free will and intellect, but always with the full awareness that this free will and intellect is actually being lived by Consciousness.

It is like a burnt rope that appears but cannot bind; it looks just like a rope but you can't tie anything up with it.

JIVATMA AND PARAMATMA

The life in me, the Jivatma, is one with the life in all, the Paramatma.

What is this life in me? It is Identified Consciousness, Impersonal Consciousness identified with this body.

It is that which is making this body breathe, and without which this body would be a corpse. Therefore, the best way to be aware of this life in me is to be aware of the breath that is going on in this body. When consciously aware of the breath, I am consciously aware of this life in me, the Jivatma, which again is the life in all – the Paramatma.

If it were not this same life within all living beings, then all of the other living beings would immediately become corpses and disintegrate into nothingness. It is the same life again that is in all of the so-called 'inanimate' things. Without this life that is present in them, they too would instantly disintegrate and disappear. The Presence of this life makes all of them appear, and in its absence they would instantaneously vanish. This life is Consciousness.

Just as the breath in the body is the evidence of this life in me, the Jivatma, the thoughts that are constantly present in the mind are also evidence of this life in me, the Jivatma.

Without the life in this body, how can there be thoughts? How can there be thoughts in a corpse? Therefore, when we pay attention to these thoughts we pay attention to the life that is there, to the Jivatma. It is in the Jivatma, or Identified Consciousness, that thoughts rise and set, and it is the Jivatma that is the content of those thoughts.

Of course life is still there in the absence of thought, such as in deep sleep, in a coma, in Samadhi, or in the miniscule period between thoughts. This is when life is Unicity; it only becomes duality with the onset of thought. But, whether thoughts are present or not, life still continues in the living body in the form of the breath.

Moreover, Consciousness is *always* there. It is there even before appearing as the life in the body, and it still remains even after departing from the body again. In fact, it is the body and all of the other objects that appear and disappear within it.

Life forever remains, beyond time and space, in the Infinite Here and Eternal Now.

Life is Consciousness.

PRESENCE PRIOR TO THOUGHT

"Who am I?"

The ego asks this question, which is a thought. It gets the answer, also in thought: "I AM."

Since the answer is in thought, the ego arises as the subject end of that thought, as 'I'. The object end is 'AM'.

What I *really* AM, my true nature, is prior to thought. Therefore, there is no ego in my true nature.

Thus, the thought-free answer to the question "Who am I?" is AM – as one is always aware of one's Existence without having to think about it. What the ego gets as an answer can only be a pointer to that Pure Presence prior to thought, the Impersonal Awareness or Consciousness in which all thoughts rise and set.

When I speak of Understanding, I speak of understanding my true nature, understanding who I AM – not what I merely *think* I am.

Here I am as this human being, identified with this human body. How is this AM related to this body? It is related to this body in a very direct and simple way: it is the life within the body. When life departs from this body appearance, the body will disappear in due course after first appearing for a time as a corpse.

The I AM, or life, proclaims its presence in the body in the form of breath. Breath will be there so long as life or Presence is there in the body appearance.

The simplest and most direct way to come into awareness of one's true nature is to direct one's attention to one's breath and thoughts.

One directs one's attention to the breath with the understanding that the breath signifies the presence of Presence in the body appearance.

Likewise when thoughts arise, one directs one's attention

to them with understanding and thus becomes aware of the Presence that is the content of all thoughts.

CONSCIOUSNESS IS
ALWAYS AWARE OF ITSELF

'Living', as the ego knows it, consists of breath in the body and thoughts in the mind.

When the ego pays attention to the breath, while understanding that the life that animates the body is the source of the breath, then the ego becomes one with that life. Life is Consciousness.

When the ego pays attention to its thoughts, while understanding that it is itself a part of those thoughts, that it is not the creator but the creation of those thoughts, and that all thoughts arise and set within the Consciousness that is thought's content, then the ego becomes one with that Consciousness.

While contemplating in this manner, we are continuously in touch consciously with Consciousness.

We are consciously in touch with Consciousness when we pay attention with this understanding to our breathing. And then, the moment our attention gets diverted by thoughts the realization arises that Consciousness is the very content of those thoughts. With this understanding, whether our attention is on the breath or on the thoughts, we remain continuously in touch consciously with Consciousness throughout our contemplation.

In this way, we become aware that Consciousness is *always* aware of itself.

THOUGHT AND AWARENESS

The content of a wave is water.

A wave as a wave is an illusion, because waves are only forms of water within the water.

A wave as water is the truth.

The content of a thought is Awareness.

A thought as a thought is an illusion, as thoughts are only forms of Awareness within Awareness.

A thought as Awareness is the Truth.

As thoughts as Awareness rise and set within that very Awareness, the illusion of the ego is created by those thoughts as the subject end of every thought.

Therefore, thought as thought can never be the Truth but only a pointer to the Truth I AM.

We can never know or be aware of the Truth objectively. We can only *be* the Truth.

We can have our concepts of the Truth and our pointers towards the Truth, but we can never know the Truth as something different from what we are.

We *are* the Truth.

LIFE IS A BELIEF SYSTEM

Life cannot be lived except under a belief system.

I get up from the bed in the morning because I believe I can easily do so. If I had been hypnotized to believe that I was extremely sick and weak, I would not be able to get up.

As human beings we all live under a common belief system:

We believe, 'I am a person with a particular name'.

We believe, 'I have the free will to decide what I want to do and to do it'.

We believe, 'I am this body and will die when the life leaves this body'.

We believe, 'I am the doer of the acts that take place through my body. I am the thinker of the thoughts that pass through my mind. I am the experiencer of the emotions and feelings that pass through my heart'.

We therefore identify with our body, thoughts, emotions, and feelings, thus forming our self-image of them.

We believe, 'I am separate from other people and have to protect myself from them'.

We believe, 'I am responsible and accountable for my actions, thoughts, and feelings, and so are other people similarly accountable for their actions, thoughts, and feelings'.

We believe, 'What happens to me is the result of either my own actions or the actions of other people, except for acts of nature'.

We believe, 'I deserve praise for the good things that I have done, but must resent myself and feel guilty for the bad things I have done. Other people equally deserve either praise or condemnation for *their* good and bad deeds'.

The list could go on and on...

What Advaita does is to offer us an alternative set of beliefs upon which our lives can be based, for our own immeasurable benefit, by tuning us in to the truth about who and what we are and thereby revealing the illusion behind what we'd mistakenly *thought* we are.

First and foremost Advaita tells us:
We are not the body. WE ARE THAT that is aware of the body yet independent of it.

Advaita tells us:
The body is only a vehicle we use for the duration of its journey from birth to death. Though the body was born and will die, what we ARE is beyond birth and death.

Advaita tells us:
We are that Impersonal Consciousness or Awareness in which all bodies including our own, as well as all of the other objects in the manifestation, appear and disappear.

Advaita tells us:
As human beings we do not live but are being lived by the Consciousness that we actually are.

Advaita tells us:

As human beings we are only appearances of Consciousness in Consciousness, like waves are forms of water within the water itself. The waves are being moved by the water that is their content, just as we are being lived by the Consciousness that is our content and whose appearances we are.

Advaita gives us the most fundamental yet profound belief system there could ever possibly be:

What we truly are is that Impersonal Consciousness, the only Presence, the only Knowledge, the only Power, beyond time and space, the Eternal Now and the Infinite Here.

Consciousness is all, as all.

Consciousness IS...

ALL IN THE MIND

The other day during the interval of a music program, I happened to meet a casual acquaintance. He said he was not hungry because he had started from home with a big glass of strong black coffee, with plenty of sugar. When I replied that what he had taken was very acidic, he told me that it was nothing of the sort: "This acidic business is *all in the mind.*"

I don't know what came over me but I found myself telling him that his statement was a very deep expression of Advaita, though I wondered whether he understood the significance of what he'd just said.

I went on to explain that the fact that we appeared to be standing in front of each other and talking to each other in flesh and blood was also in the mind, being ultimately only a thought within the mind. In fact the whole Universe, including the two of us, was nothing more than a thought within the mind, within Consciousness, Consciousness being all there truly is.

He gave me a strange look, and I could almost feel him taking a step backwards. I don't know what compelled me to talk to him like that, but its spontaneity only confirmed for me once again that we do not live but are being lived by Consciousness in Consciousness as its appearances.

In fact, this is precisely what Nisargadatta Maharaj used to say in his talks:

"Here I am talking and there you are listening. What is actually happening is that Consciousness is speaking to Consciousness, and Consciousness is listening to Consciousness... Consciousness is all there is."

THE EGO IS A THOUGHT

The ego is itself but a thought.

How can one thought 'think' another thought?

'I am the thinker' is a thought. How can this thought think another thought *and* be the thinker thought?

'I am the doer of this act' is a thought. How can a thought be the doer of an action?

'This deed has been done' is yet another thought. But, can a thought be a deed?

'I am doing this action' is a thought.

'This action' is only a part of the thought, the object part, rising and setting in Consciousness with Consciousness as its content.

'I am doing' is the subject part of the thought, rising and setting in Consciousness with Consciousness as its content.

Consciousness is the content of all thought, just as Consciousness is our content – 'we' being but parts of a thought.

Consciousness is all there is. Consciousness is all we are.

UNWANTED THOUGHTS
IN MEDITATION

If while sitting for meditation a lot of unwanted thoughts or memories intrude in our minds, creating equally unwanted emotions that disturb our peace, how are we to deal with such thoughts and emotions?

Let us employ the analogy of the windscreen of a car that we are driving through the rain. If the rain falling on the windscreen is disturbing our clear view, what we do is to look through the rain and blurry water on the window to make out the road ahead.

In the same way, when memory-thoughts intrude in our meditation, creating unwanted emotions that obscure our 'view', what we do is to look through the emotions (the blurry rain) to the pure I AM that is always there as the substratum of our existence (the road ahead).

In the process, we will realize that the I AM is the very content of the thoughts and emotions that arise and set within it, including the thoughts that have given rise to our present emotions. Thereby, our thoughts and emotions will automatically merge with the I AM.

And then we will find that WE ARE the rain, the window, the thoughts, the emotions, the peace... as well as 'the road ahead'.

Once this clear Understanding is there our meditation becomes deeper.

ONE WATER

I.

If a large mass of water were to spontaneously become 'aware' of itself, it would become aware of itself through its form as the ocean.

Whenever waves would appear in that ocean, the water would become identified with those waves as 'identified water' within each separate wave.

The water within each would thus appear restricted to the separate form of each wave, yet would really remain the same undifferentiated water all the while.

Each individual wave might 'think' it is living its own life separate from the other waves, but would always actually remain just a gesture within the wide expanse of ocean water; and all of the other 'separate' waves would equally be nothing but gestures within that same water that is the essence of *all* waves.

Thus, we might say *the ocean is 'living' the life of the waves.*

II.

When Impersonal Consciousness suddenly becomes aware of itself – I AM – it becomes aware of itself through its form as the manifestation.

When beings and objects appear within the manifestation, Impersonal Consciousness identifies with those beings and objects translating itself into the Identified Consciousness within each one.

Impersonal Consciousness, as Identified Consciousness, identifies with each appearance, object, or being, yet actually remains Pure Impersonal Consciousness all the while.

Each appearance, whether object or being, 'believes' it is living its own life separate from the other objects and beings but it is actually Impersonal Consciousness, in the form of the Identified Consciousness within each object or being, that is living the life of those appearances until such time as those appearances last.

They all actually remain mere forms and gestures within Impersonal Consciousness.

All of the separate appearances are truly nothing but the one Impersonal Consciousness that is their essence.

III.

This human body has appeared within Impersonal Consciousness as a part of the manifestation, and Impersonal Consciousness has identified with this body as Identified Consciousness.

This Identified Consciousness has thus conceptually restricted itself to this particular body appearance, and thus *conceives* of itself as a human being...

But, it is always actually Pure Impersonal Consciousness all the while.

I am now a human being, an ego, apparently 'living' my own life separate and distinct from the other human beings and objects within the manifestation, but it is really Impersonal Consciousness, translated into Identified Consciousness identified with this particular body, that is actually living 'my' life.

Moreover, it is the same Impersonal Consciousness that is equally the essence of all of the other appearances — appearing as them and living their lives.

We are separate in appearance but one in essence.

IV.

The Identified Consciousness identified with the body also identifies with the different states of the body:

In the waking state, it takes the form of the waking ego in the waking world.

In the dream state, it takes the form of a dream ego within a dream world.

In the deep sleep state, where it is not even aware of itself, there is no ego, no world, no thoughts, etc.

However, the body continues to live breath by breath, and the Identified Consciousness therefore still continues.

The man of Understanding is aware that he is actually Pure Consciousness identified with the body appearance.

It is the body appearance that is subject to birth and death, and along with it the ego that belongs to it.

When the body dies, Identified Consciousness and the ego will 'die' as well, but Impersonal Consciousness always remains:

The Infinite Here... The Eternal Now... I AM.

TWO SIDES OF THE SAME COIN

"I AM."

Impersonal Consciousness, identified with the body as Identified Consciousness, is the content of this thought.

Impersonal Consciousness and Identified Consciousness are not separate or independent things, just as the actor and the role played are not living in different human bodies.

The actor appears as the role but never actually becomes another character. Role or no role, he still always remains the actor.

Similarly, Impersonal Consciousness always remains Impersonal Consciousness, even when appearing as Identified Consciousness identified within a body.

Impersonal Consciousness abides in Unicity and only appears as Identified Consciousness in duality. However, Unicity and duality are two sides of the same coin, always together. One cannot *be* without the other.

As long as the mind is there taking delivery of thoughts, it is there as Identified Consciousness in the form of the ego.

Only when the mind is completely at rest, such as when the mind lingers between two thoughts or settles into the thought-free state of Turiya, does Identified Consciousness become a pure reflection of Impersonal Consciousness.

However, it's important to understand that Impersonal Consciousness and Identified Consciousness are actually the same thing: the actor as himself and the actor playing a role.

The realization "I AM" is that of Identified Consciousness conceptually disengaging from its attachment to the body and the manifestation, thereby reorienting itself to the Impersonal Consciousness that it always actually was.

It is Identified Consciousness recognizing its true identity as Impersonal Consciousness: I AM, as opposed to I am this or that.

Therefore when Identified Consciousness is consciously aware of itself, not as the ego or the body but solely as Pure Identified Consciousness alone, it is then also consciously aware of itself as Impersonal Consciousness.

THE MOST POWERFUL THOUGHT

With the proper Understanding, the greatest and most powerful thought in the world is the thought, "I ... AM."

Here, the subject end of the thought 'I', the ego, the Identified Consciousness, is directed inwards towards its Source – the object end of the thought 'AM', which is Impersonal Consciousness, the Source of all there is.

Both the subject end of the thought, the ego or Identified Consciousness, and the object end of the thought, Impersonal Consciousness, are parts of the same thought. They also both represent the same one Consciousness.

The thought "I AM," with the proper Understanding, brings about the merging of the Identified Consciousness 'I' with the Impersonal Consciousness 'AM'. "I ... AM."

Amazingly this most profound thought in English, "I AM," bears a great resemblance to the most powerful sound in Sanskrit, AUM.

When Impersonal Consciousness gets reflected in the body as the life in the body appearance, it is covered over by the three states of the body. As Identified Consciousness it becomes the substratum of the three states – the waking state, the dreaming state, and the deep sleep state:

A = Waking State.
U = Dreaming State.
M = Deep Sleep State.
MMMMM = Pure Identified Consciousness.

When we utter the word AUM with Understanding, our attention is directed to the Identified Consciousness that is the substratum MMMMM of the three states of the body, through which the body is lived.

Thus, the last M continues in a humming sound: MMMMM... representing 'AM'.

The word AUM also encompasses the full spectrum of sounds that we make in order to be able to talk:

A = Sound that comes from the throat.

U = Sound that comes from the middle of the mouth.

M = Sound that comes from the front of the mouth, the lips

Therefore, the one word AUM is the template of all of the sounds we use in order to think or communicate.

It therefore encompasses our entire conceptual world in thought, as well as pointing towards our true nature prior to thought, and thus represents both our assumed identity, 'I', *and* our true Identity, 'AM'.

MMMMM... the Pure Identified Consciousness that is the substratum of the three states of the body through which our lives are lived:

I AM – AUM.

INTENTION

We do not live but we are being lived by Consciousness, or the Source.

More specifically, we are being lived through our intentions. But, just as we do not know what thoughts will come into our minds next, we equally don't know what intentions will come into our minds next in the form of thoughts.

Whatever we do or don't do is the result of our intentions.

We may say we intended to do one thing yet ended up doing something else, but this isn't really correct. We may indeed have intended to do the first thing, but what we ultimately did was exactly what we most intended at that particular time.

We may not have wanted to become a doctor when we were younger, yet somehow we still ended up being a doctor. Clearly, whatever we did to become a doctor we ultimately did because we finally *intended* to do so.

We do not do anything unless we intend to do it, whether we know it or not.

However, our intentions are truly not in our hands. We're clearly being lived to have an intention just as we are being lived to have any other thought.

Therefore do whatever you want to freely, with awareness, in the utter conviction that you want to do it because you are supposed to do it.

The consequences of your actions are clearly not in your hands. Therefore accept them as they are, trusting that they're meant to be exactly that way.

If you want something, then know that you have been given the intention to want it.

If you want to do something, then know that you've been given the intention to do it.

If you have the intention to do it yet find you don't act upon it, that is because you have later been given the intention to *not* do it.

With this Understanding, you can always be at peace with your intentions.

CONSCIOUSNESS IS OUR CONTENT

Off and on through the course of the day, let me look around myself in conscious awareness of Consciousness. Let me see myself, and all of the other human beings, as nothing but appearances of Consciousness in Consciousness, with Consciousness as our content.

Let me see this table, this chair, these curtains, these walls, this carpet, this floor, as nothing but appearances of Consciousness in Consciousness, with Consciousness as their content.

Let me be aware of how as mere appearances we were not there earlier, we *are* here now, and in the course of time we will disappear once again. We come from Consciousness, we appear within Consciousness, and we will eventually disappear back into Consciousness again. We are thus all nothing but Consciousness.

Let me be grateful that this witnessing is happening through me, according to the intention of Consciousness. And, let me recognize that I am presently feeling grateful only because, according to Consciousness, I am supposed to be feeling grateful.

Consciousness is all there is.

WHERE DID THE FLAME
COME FROM?

Sometimes, Nisargadatta Maharaj would strike a match stick to light a flame. "Where did the flame come from?" he would ask.

Certain conditions took place where a match stick with the appropriate chemicals soaked into it was struck on the side of a match box, and a flame appeared.

Having appeared, the match stick became the "food-body" of that flame. The flame would last so long as the match stick was there as its 'food', and when the match stick was consumed the flame disappeared.

Where did the flame come from and where did the flame disappear to?

The flame was an appearance of Consciousness in

Consciousness, and the flame disappeared back again into that very Consciousness that it was an appearance of.

In the same way, I appeared as this human being when certain conditions took place within the manifestation that allowed for the formation of a human being to occur.

This human body is now the 'food' of the I AM. This I AM, or Identified Consciousness, will only continue for as long as this "food-body" sustains it.

It will cease when the 'chemical of life' within the body appearance has been burned up, and then the knowledge that I AM will disappear once again... but...

Impersonal Consciousness always remains beneath.

LOVE AND GRATITUDE

I.

When one realizes that all of these apparently separate appearances are nothing but the one Pure Consciousness that I AM, then that realization of Oneness is Pure Love.

Love is the acceptance of our Oneness, as opposed to the belief in our apparent separation.

With that acceptance, we start each day with love:

We radiate love to ourselves and feel radiant with love.

We radiate love to our family, to our near and dear ones, to our friends and acquaintances, and bless them and are one with them.

We radiate love to everyone – including those whom we may dislike, including those whom we do not even know – and bless them and are one with them.

We radiate love to everything – to this whole world and everything in it, to this entire manifestation with all of its contents – as our very Selves, as Consciousness.

We feel our Oneness with everything and everyone as that One Consciousness, that One Love that is above and beyond all external happenings, and we *are* that Love.

The secret essence behind the attitude of love is the realization that God, or Consciousness, is all there is. If God is all there is, then we are nothing but God appearing as us; and, this world is nothing but God appearing as this world.

There is just one Actor playing all of the roles in the movie of life, and that Actor is Pure Love. If we perceive others as God appearing as them, and ourselves as God appearing as us, then can the attitude of love towards all be anything but the natural outcome?

11.

Gratitude is as important as love.

Let us look at all that has happened in our lives with deep gratitude, and thank God for it.

The greatest thing that has happened is our being blessed with the Understanding of our true nature. Let us give thanks, for true Understanding is very precious and rare. Nothing could ever be more valuable than that.

Let us thank God for our family, our relations, our friends, our work, our home and belongings, and our health such as it is, our bodies, etc. Let us be filled with gratitude for all.

In this way, may we not take any of God's endless bounty for granted.

Let us look upon all of the happenings of life with gratitude, no matter what they may be. Beyond the confusion of positive and negative, may we experience every single moment with deep gratitude for our very Being.

Love and gratitude are the fruits of the tree of Understanding. Let us pray that we may be continually lived with the attitude of love and gratitude.

THERE ARE NOT TWO PRESENCES

The most fundamental concept of Advaita is that Consciousness is all, as all; God is all, as all. The manifestation is nothing but Consciousness.

This is Advaita.

It is Consciousness or God *in* me and in this table, in this plastic, in this event, in this circumstance, etc.

It is Consciousness *as* me and as this table, as this plastic, as this event, as this circumstance, etc.

Consciousness is the only Power, the only Presence, the only Knowledge.

There are not two powers; there are not two presences.

Therefore, there is no good or bad: no good power vs. evil power, no good presence vs. evil presence, no good knowledge vs. evil knowledge.

Because the whole manifestation and everything in it is nothing but an appearance of Consciousness in Consciousness, there is no power in any of the appearances.

Ultimately, the highest good and the worst evil are only appearances, and an appearance by itself can clearly only be an illusion, whether seen on the screen of the theatre or the screen of Consciousness.

We may sympathize with the role of the hero and condemn that of the villain, but deep down we know they're both just characters created according to the storyline of the film.

We may suffer the 'existence' of evil in the world and enjoy that of goodness, but our difficulties arise when we take those appearances as real and forget the Consciousness in which they appear, i.e. when we take the *role* as real and forget the Actor.

Immediately we give appearances the power of good and

evil we posit the existence of multiple presences, thus forgetting that the only true Power is Consciousness, the only true Presence is Consciousness, and the only true Knowledge is Consciousness.

Consciousness, or God, is truly all there is.

BE STILL AND KNOW THAT
I AM GOD

The Presence that you are is not an object in the mind. Presence is beyond the mind because the mind is nothing but thought arising within Presence. One can become aware of Presence, of the Consciousness that one is, when one is still, having let go of thought and its creation, the ego.

When you are aware of your thoughts, try to notice the Consciousness in which the thoughts arise and set. Know that you are doing this because you are being lived to do so.

We are always the Presence, the Awareness in which all else arises, but we are not always consciously aware of it. The water is aware of its waves but the waves forget they're just shapes within the water. They only become more deeply aware upon realizing that they *are* the water.

Every time a thought arises, observe it and realize that

you are not this thought but that in which it has arisen, the Presence, the Awareness that you *are*. You are not the ego created by your thoughts.

"Be still and know that I am God."

Ironically, the highest effort or Sadhana we can do is to let go and be aware of the Awareness that we are.

POINTER TO THE TRUTH

"Who am I?"
Who is asking this question?

Impersonal Consciousness identified with the body appearance as Identified Consciousness, in its role as the ego, is asking this question.

This question is a thought in which the ego, in other words the identification with the body as the subject end of that thought, is itself an intrinsic part.

However, I AM is not a thought. It is that Pure Awareness in which all there is rises and sets – *as* thought.

In Pure Awareness, the ego vanishes as a shadow vanishes in the direct light of the midday sun.

Therefore, concerning the question "Who am I?" -

The answer-in-thought, "I AM," can only be a pointer to that Truth that is prior to all thought and thus prior to the one asking the question, because the Truth cannot be objectified by the ego, which is but a thought within it.

But fortunately, the answer, such as it is, can point *towards* Understanding by making the ego aware of its true identity as Impersonal Consciousness.

As Impersonal Consciousness, I AM all there is.
I AM the Infinite Here, the Eternal Now.

However, the mirage of the human being continues and will continue breath by breath in the body, thought by thought in the mind, till such time as 'life' remains.

In the meantime:

As Ramesh said – May we remain continuously connected with the Source, through the total Understanding and Acceptance that we do not live but are being lived.

And, as Nisargadatta Maharaj said – May our attention

be repeatedly directed towards the I AM, the Impersonal Consciousness that we *are*... until it remains there.

Ultimately, Advaita in daily living boils down to these two things.

THE DIVINE MOVIE IS
ALREADY IN THE CAN

Sri Nisargadatta Maharaj used to say that the manifestation is like a movie in which the Producer, the Script Writer, the Director, the Cameraman, the full cast, and also the audience are all Consciousness itself! Ramesh, who often referred to this concept used to say, "The movie is already in the can."

Actually, the analogy is extremely helpful in understanding that we do not live 'our life' but that life is being lived through us by Consciousness. As appearances of Consciousness in Consciousness we are all simply roles in this Divine Movie, just characters with a supposed free will and intellect.

With this Understanding we live our lives fully, using our apparent free will and intellect to try to fulfill our desires, wants, and dreams, to bring about the improvements we so long for in life and in the process we experience our frustrations, our angers, our victories, our joys, and our sorrows.

We live our lives to the full but all the while KNOWING that whatever we do, whatever we feel, and whatever we experience has already been filmed, and "the film is already in the can."

This *Knowing* helps us avoid any anxiety over the results of 'our' actions as we are able to work efficiently with the "working mind," as Ramesh called it, without the "thinking mind" interfering and worrying over the imagined results of the work at hand.

This knowledge empowers us to live life passionately with great freedom, accepting life as it unfolds before us, no matter how.

Far from paralyzing our sense of volition it frees us from the fear of using it fully, through the faith that whatever we are 'doing' is exactly what we are meant to be doing. Through the equanimity it invokes, it grounds us in deep peace and trust.

While watching a movie, we know that it has already been fully filmed. But, as the story unfolds before us we identify with the characters therein, suffering and enjoying life along with them, even though we know that what we are seeing isn't actually real.

Is the 'movie' of our own lives really any different? As human beings, we are just illusory roles in this movie. Only the Actor is real.

The Divine Movie that is 'our life' is already in the can!

THE TRIAD

When a thought arises in Identified Consciousness, the thought has its two ends in duality: the subject end (the ego) and the object end (the manifestation). The thought creates the two ends, and Identified Consciousness is the content of both. The ego and the manifestation that the thought is concerned with do not exist independently or of themselves; they are just parts of the thought.

In short, with every thought a triad is formed between its subject, its object, and its content ('me', 'that', and the Consciousness they appear within – i.e. 'me', 'that', and THAT). Therefore, the entire manifestation, along with whoever and whatever appears or happens within it, is nothing but Identified Consciousness:

Seeing thought – seer and seen have no separate existence.

Doing thought — doer and deed have no separate existence.

Hearing thought — hearer and heard have no separate existence, etc.

They are all just parts of a thought.

THE HUMAN BEING THAT
I THINK I AM

WHO AM I?

I am a human being whose name is xyz. I am strong and healthy. I am intelligent and of good character, with free will to do whatever I want to do. I have a good reputation and am reasonably comfortable in life. I have a good family and also have some wonderful friends. I have a good job, etc.

How am I able to state all of these things?

Obviously, because this is what I think about myself. It means that these are all thoughts about 'me'.

Where do all these thoughts arise?

Obviously, in my Consciousness.

That means that if I am not conscious, as when I am in deep sleep or a coma where there are no thoughts, then I will not know who I am at all.

This means that it is these thoughts that rise and set in Consciousness that tell me who I am.

That means that it is Consciousness, which is the content of my thoughts, that really tells me who I am.

This therefore means that I am nothing but Consciousness prior to thought, the Impersonal Awareness that I AM, in which all thoughts rise and set.

But then, if I truly am Impersonal Consciousness, how do I have this body and this ego or personality separate from all of the other egos and objects?

This can only be explained with further concepts:

When a body is born or takes life in the manifestation – the *Dream of Consciousness* – Impersonal Consciousness gets reflected in that body and gets identified with it as Identified Consciousness, the reflected I AM.

This reflected I AM gets identified with each body whenever a body/mind organism forms, just as the one true sun in the sky gets reflected in several puddles at once, each forming reflected suns on the surface of their waters.

An ego associated with each body is then continually formed as the subject end of every movement of thought that arises within each Identified Consciousness, the object end depending upon the nature of the thought.

Prior to the arising of thought, or in the interval between thoughts, I AM Pure Identified Consciousness. I only become the ego with the arising of thought. Impersonal Consciousness is the content of this thought, just as sunlight is the content of each reflected sun appearing within every puddle.

As long as there is life in the body, thoughts will be there creating this ego – in reference to which I described myself earlier. Therefore, I *think* I am this human being with its free will, intellect, and sense of personal doership.

This human being that I think I am, as well as all of the other human beings and objects in the manifestation, is nothing but a role played by Impersonal Consciousness in this Divine Drama, or *Dream of Consciousness.*

As long as this role is there, it can never be separated from its true content and true identity as Impersonal Consciousness. Although my appearance as this role will eventually end, Consciousness will always remain.

I am therefore always one with Consciousness.

DEALING WITH HAPPENINGS

It so happens that xyz, whom I had trusted, has cheated me:

The first thing is to accept the happening.

The second thing is to de-personalize the happening by differentiating xyz from the cheating.

I simply accept the fact that xyz does not live but is only *being* lived, and in this moment he is being lived to cheat me. He is a part of the happening, in Consciousness, but is not the cause of the happening.

The third thing is to deal with the actual situation itself.

It is a happening that I'm losing some money and I naturally work towards limiting the damage.

As for the future, I know that xyz is not being lived to be trustworthy and will thus take care when dealing with him.

When I'm walking on slippery ground, I don't blame the ground, I just take care.

It so happens that someone has been rude and insulting towards you:

That person has only been lived to do so as part of the happening; he is not the cause or the source of the happening.

Why unnecessarily waste energy in anger, hurt, or hatred against him? The resulting calmness is bound to have a positive effect on the situation and 'the person' in question.

In this way, the entire event will simply pass away without any negative after-effects.

It so happens that I've not worked hard enough and thus fail in my exams:

Knowing that I have been lived to be lazy, I feel no shame or guilt.

I learn from this event that if I want to succeed I must work harder the next time, but I also realize that whether I succeed in working harder or not is entirely beyond my control.

In this way, although I may feel disappointed over my exam results, I feel no particular tension about it.

As Ramesh suggested, all of our experiences in life are really nothing more than happenings. The persons connected with the happenings, including ourselves, are really just a part of the happenings – not the cause of them.

True Understanding of this de-personalizes one's life experiences by differentiating the persons apparently 'doing' the actions from the actual events themselves.

This results in an absence of negative personal emotions, which allows the happenings of life to be dealt with objectively.

THE SUPREME PRAYER
OF THE EGO

May I be lived more and more in Conscious Awareness
of Impersonal Consciousness appearing as me,
while there is life in this body.

May I be lived in Conscious Awareness
of Impersonal Consciousness appearing as me,
while life is leaving the body.

THOUGHT IS DUALITY

The Truth is prior to thought; it is that in which thought rises and sets. The Truth is Unicity; thought is duality.

Only when thought merges back into Truth does duality become Unicity, and then there is no thought and no one to *know* the Truth.

The ego, as an aspect of thought, can never know the Truth; it can only disappear into the Truth.

A drop of water can never know the ocean; it can only disappear into the ocean.

The moment we enter the world of thought, we have 'emerged' from Unicity into duality.

But the moment thought fully sets, like the sun

disappearing over the horizon, we dissolve again into the ocean of Truth.

THIS THAT I AM

In every human being there are two aspects:
1. This that I AM.
2. This that I *think* I am.

Except for a miniscule minority, the majority of human beings are only concerned with 'this that I think I am'. To them, this is the same as 'This that I AM'. 'This that I think I am' is in total control of their lives from birth to death while 'This that I AM' is buried deep within, unclaimed and unknown.

Every human being, like everything else in this world, is under sentence of death from the moment it is born. All life as we know it is an unceasing journey, beginning with birth, which is constantly on the move day in and day out towards the destination of death.

As stated above, only a tiny minority are enlivened to undertake the search of discovery for the Godhead buried deep within.

'This that I think I am' is a belief system:

I believe and accept that I am a personality, an individual, an ego.

I have a human body and therefore I believe and accept that I am a human being, having identified myself with this body.

I believe and accept that I'm tall or short, fat or thin, and so on.

I believe and accept that I have free will to choose and decide what I want to do, as well as an intellect to help me make those decisions.

I therefore believe that I am the doer of my actions and thus accept responsibility for them.

In other words, 'this that I think I am' is a belief system based upon a collection of thoughts!

I think I am the thinker of my thoughts and the doer of my deeds.

I think I am a person, an individual with a name and form.

I think that I was born and that I will one day die.

However, when I am in deep sleep or unconscious and there is no thought, where is this world, this body, and this individual ego then? They disappear into Consciousness.

Upon waking up, thoughts reappear once again and this world, this body, and this ego also reappear.

Therefore it's obvious that they all only 'exist' in the realm of thought: they are just a belief system that is based in thought.

Where do thoughts rise and set? Obviously, within Consciousness.

When Consciousness is at rest there are no thoughts. Therefore, Awareness or Consciousness is the content of all thoughts, just as water is the content of the waves that rise and set in the ocean.

'This that I *think* I am' is a human being, an ego, who is a part of this world and manifestation, all of which only 'exists' within the construct of thought.

'This that I AM' is Pure Awareness, in which thought rises and sets, and which is the very content of all thought.

Therefore, even while I think I am a human being, a part of this manifestation, living in this world, I am always actually that Pure Awareness or Consciousness that is the content of this, and all, thought.

To repeat: what I AM is Pure Awareness, Consciousness, or Presence prior to thought – THAT in which all thought rises and sets.

This is Unicity.

When thought arises it gives birth to duality, the world of opposites: good and bad, male and female, beautiful and ugly, courage and fear, health and disease, me and you, and so on.

Each arising thought has its two ends: the subject end or ego, and the object end, which must obviously be a part of the manifestation.

Manifestation means duality.

Pure Awareness, or Consciousness, means Unicity.

Thought is the medium through which Unicity becomes duality, through which 'This that I AM' becomes 'this that I think I am'.

IMPERSONAL CONSCIOUSNESS AND IDENTIFIED CONSCIOUSNESS

"I AM."

Impersonal Consciousness identified with the body as Identified Consciousness is the content of this thought.

However, Impersonal Consciousness and Identified Consciousness are not two different things. The actor and the role are not two different people. The actor only appears as a role but is never actually that role. He still always remains the actor.

Similarly, Impersonal Consciousness always actually remains Impersonal Consciousness, whether it is appearing as Identified Consciousness identified with a body or not.

Impersonal Consciousness remains in Unicity and only *appears* as Identified Consciousness in duality, but Unicity and duality are really two sides of the same coin, always together.

So long as the mind is there it is always arising within the Identified Consciousness I AM, even when one is consciously aware of *being* that Consciousness.

Furthermore, it is only when the mind is completely at rest, as in deep sleep or in the thought-free state of Turiya, that Identified Consciousness remains a pure reflection of Impersonal Consciousness; but, it is important to understand that Impersonal Consciousness and Identified Consciousness are always actually the same in essence.

The realization that "I AM," which is dependent upon the existence of the living body, can only appear within Identified Consciousness in the form of a thought.

This realization is the Identified Consciousness conceptually realizing its true identity as Impersonal Consciousness, independent of the body or the manifestation.

As long as the body/mind unit is there it is impossible to go beyond the mind, because being oneself a mere thought one obviously cannot go beyond thought.

One *can* consciously be aware of oneself as the 'life' living the body as the Identified Consciousness "I AM," but it will always still be only as a thought.

THOUGHTS ARE NOT
THE TRUTH

Our life is basically and fundamentally lived through the senses of the body, and most thoughts are basically just the output of those senses.

All of our senses are by their very nature extremely limited. We can see only a fraction of the things that can be seen, and hear only a fraction of the sounds that can be heard, etc. Therefore, our so-called 'reality' is truly a fraud because it consists of nothing more than the input of these unfathomably limited senses. And therefore, what we call our 'life', which consists of nothing but thoughts based entirely upon our senses, is also really just an illusion, like a dream.

What is thought? It is a movement in Consciousness, just as a wave is a movement in water. In our case as human beings, the Consciousness in which thought arises is

Identified Consciousness, that is, Consciousness identified with a body appearance that has appeared within Consciousness itself. The thoughts or movements in that Consciousness are obviously then always identified with that particular body appearance, thereby creating the ego as the subject end of each arising thought. Those thoughts in turn are entirely the product of the senses of the body, which are by their very nature incapable of perceiving even 1% of what is potentially there to be perceived. What then shall we make of the so called 'reality' of the ego?

What we human beings experience as 'life' isn't reality or truth. Our sense impressions are only miniscule fragments of reality, and we should take them as such. What we appear to be is based upon the blurry world of imagination and dream while what we *really* are is the Truth, that one Truth that no one can deny – I AM, existence prior to sensory based thought.

As human beings we are part of this manifestation, but is the manifestation actually real? How are we even aware of this world that we 'live' in? We are only aware of the manifestation through sensory based thought. Thoughts inform us about the manifestation, and about ourselves and our place within it. Since thoughts can only arise and set within Consciousness, and are composed entirely of Consciousness, Consciousness must be the true content of both the manifestation and the ego.

Our senses can only tell us about the appearance of things. Therefore, let us always remember that what our senses report is an illusion while what the Understanding reports makes us aware of the Truth behind the illusion. Our senses, being solely based on the *appearance* of life, speak to us of the existence of two powers: good and evil, heaven and hell, beautiful and ugly, etc. – in other words duality. The Understanding on the other hand testifies to the Existence of the one true Power, the one Presence, the one Truth – Consciousness, or Awareness prior to sensory based thought.

Our senses function within the realm of time and space. The report of the senses regarding the various individuals or circumstances that are encountered in life is thus always continually changing. What was not there before is here now, and what is appearing here now will not be there later.

However, that one Pure Consciousness that we 'see' through the eyes of Understanding remains eternally unchanging.

When thoughts are based on sensory evidence, they are based in time and space and are therefore not the Truth. Only that 'thought' that is prior to sensory testimony – I AM, PEACE, LOVE, ETERNITY, TRUTH – is beyond time and space, and is a direct expression of REALITY.

NO PAST LIVES IN ADVAITA

When we refer to past lives in Advaita, we do not refer to the past lives of a soul going from birth to birth taking on new bodies. What we refer to is the life of a body/mind organism born in the past.

When life occurs in a body in the Divine Drama that is this manifestation, Consciousness gets reflected in the body as the awareness that I AM. This reflected I AM gets identified with that body, and an illusory ego gets created as the subject end of every thought that arises in that particular Identified Consciousness.

When life 'ends' and Consciousness ceases to be reflected in that body, the ego naturally gets extinguished. There is no question of the ego surviving the death of the body, or surviving as a soul and getting re-born in another body/mind organism.

Consciousness ceases to reflect as I AM in a dead body, and thus the corresponding ego gets extinguished along with the 'life' of the body. There are no past or future births *for the ego* in Advaita.

And that is all there is to it.

The question then arises: What about all of the wishes, desires, achievements, failures, frustrations, and so on that have taken place in the body/mind organism connected with the ego? Do they all get extinguished too?

Nothing is wasted in nature...

They all join the pool of Consciousness and are absorbed therein as parts of the mix to be used in the formation of new body/mind organisms.

Whenever a new body/mind organism gets formed, a selection from this pool gets attached to the new organism in accordance with the characteristics and nature required by its particular destiny.

It may happen that a new body/mind organism gets a large amount of the mix from one specific previous organism, and we thus think this previous 'person' or its 'soul' has been reborn. It is clearly not so.

It may also happen that some lingering thought forms, from specific egos that have 'died', may still be around in space until they are fully absorbed into the pool of Consciousness. We may know of them as spirits. However, the fact remains that they are still just appearances of Consciousness in Consciousness, and if we're aware of them at all it could only be in the notional world of thought, the content of which will also be Consciousness.

It may also happen that a new body/mind organism may receive a few memories, out of the pool of Consciousness, of happenings from the 'life' of a previous body/mind organism. We may therefore think that a previous ego or 'soul' has been re-born. However, the ego of the present body/mind organism is clearly totally different and new. It has a new name and different characteristics, and therefore has no direct relationship with the previous ego that was extinguished along with the previous 'life'.

To conclude: in Advaita, there is no soul with free will continuing from birth to birth, doing what it wants to do independent of Consciousness.

Consciousness is all there is.

THERE IS NO CREATION,
THERE IS NO DESTRUCTION

"There is no creation.
There is no destruction."

– Ramana Maharshi

Who is saying this?

I, Chaitanya Balsekar, am referring to Ramana Maharshi's statement.

When I say: "I, Chaitanya Balsekar, am saying this," it is only an expression of a thought in my mind, in other words, a thought in Consciousness. Therefore 'I' am only a thought in Consciousness. If there were no Consciousness there would be no such thought.

But this seems really odd: Here I am, with this body; I can feel and see it, hear it talk, etc., yet still maintain that I am just a thought in Consciousness!

If I say that I can touch my body, see my body and so on, what I am stating is only a thought in my mind, in Consciousness. If there were no Consciousness, there'd be no thought and where would this 'I' be then?

I am only a thought in Consciousness, rising and setting in Consciousness. You are only a thought in Consciousness, rising and setting in Consciousness. The whole manifestation is only a thought rising and setting in Consciousness. Consciousness is truly all there is.

There is no Creation. There is no Destruction.

ALL THERE IS, IS CONSCIOUSNESS.

I AM CONSCIOUSNESS, INFINITE AND ETERNAL

Consciousness is all there is, infinite and eternal, beyond the concepts of space and time.

When a body is born within the manifestation – i.e. the manifestation or *appearance* of Consciousness in Consciousness – Consciousness gets reflected in it.

That Pure Impersonal Consciousness that gets reflected within the body as Identified Consciousness remains unaffected by the constraints of that body.

It is only Identified Consciousness in its role as the illusory ego that appears affected by the body's limitations.

The ego identifies with the body and claims to be a human being, identifies with the mind and claims to be the thinker of the thoughts, the experiencer of the emotions and feelings, and the doer of the acts that take place through that body/mind organism according to its destiny.

Therefore, the ego 'feels' affected by the impediments and modifications of the body/mind.

Divine Hypnosis, or Maya, makes the ego believe it is living its life, when in reality 'its life' is being lived for it.

As the ego, I am only an *appearance* of Consciousness in Consciousness, and Consciousness is my content.

So long as I – the ego – am being lived to identify with this body, I am limited in the eternity of time to the lifetime of the body, limited in the infinity of space to the dimensions of the body.

But, as Impersonal Consciousness I am Infinite and Eternal, unborn and undying – I AM all there is.

Meanwhile, let the body/mind organism live out its allotted span according to its destiny...
...as I Abide.

I AM THIS LIFE

Life is not a challenge to be faced, but a mystery to be enjoyed as it unfolds moment by moment. Life has no purpose. Life is its own purpose, meaning 'living' is the purpose of life.

Here I am, Chaitanya Sadashiv Balsekar, a person, a human being. I appear as such because of the life that is there in this human body. If it were not for the life that is there within it this body would be a corpse, and there would be no 'person' by the name of Chaitanya Sadashiv Balsekar.

Therefore what I am is this 'life', not this human being, and this life is Consciousness. This human being is a convicted appearance of Consciousness appearing under the sentence of disappearance - it will one day disappear back into the very Consciousness it presently appears within when 'I', as its life, cease to be identified with this body. However,

I will always remain: the Infinite Here and the Eternal Now.

All that is necessary is the total Understanding that the content of each breath is Consciousness, and the content of each thought, along with its subject the ego, is also Consciousness. Consciousness is all, as all.

CONSCIOUSNESS IS.

LIFE IN THIS BODY

What am I but the life that is in this body, as this body.

Let me sit still and quietly pay attention to that life, and be aware of that life, or Consciousness, throbbing within me.

Let me pay attention to that same life that is appearing in all of these other bodies and objects in this manifestation.

Let me be quietly and consciously aware of it and my oneness with it. This life in me, the Jivatma, is one with the life in all, the Paramatma.

I AM this life in all. This life in all, I AM. The Jivatma and the Paramatma are one. I AM THAT, THAT IS 'I'.

I am not this body.

I AM the life that is in this body, as this body.

Without this life, this body would be a corpse.

It is the same life that is in all of these other people, in all of these other bodies. Without that life, all of these human bodies would be corpses.

When I see myself in the mirror, I see the life that is this face, the life that is this body.

When I see all of these other people, I am seeing the life that is in them.

When I see this table, I see the life that is this table. Without that same life, this table would immediately crumble into dust and disappear.

When I see this room, I see the life that is this room. When I see this manifestation, I see the life that is this manifestation.

When I see myself, these other people, this table, this

room, this manifestation, I see that same life that is appearing as all of us.

That life is Consciousness.

Consciousness is all, as all. Consciousness is all there is.

THE MAN OF ADVAITA

What is the difference between the way the average person lives and the way the man of Advaita lives?

The average person lives within a belief system, which tells him that he has free will, intellect, and the power to decide what he wants to do and to do it. He believes he is accountable for what he does, and that other people are likewise accountable for what they do. He feels guilty, blaming himself for his failures and negative actions, while feeling equally proud of his positive achievements. He also blames others for their 'bad' deeds, resenting or even hating them, and is usually full of envy and jealousy.

He believes that he is the doer of his acts, the thinker of his thoughts, and the experiencer of his feelings and emotions. He lives in fear and anxiety, being continually worried about the results of his endeavors. His relations with other people are full of rivalry, resentment, hatred, envy, and jealousy, with only the occasional experience of love and compassion mixed in. All the while, he is a slave to judgment – both of himself and others. His self image is that of a human being who is all alone, who must remain continually on guard to protect and defend against a world set against him.

What about the person who has a deep understanding of Advaita? The essence of his understanding being that Consciousness is all there is, his belief system is totally different:

The man of Advaita understands that just as water manifests as the wave that is its very appearance and of which it is the entire content of, Consciousness 'lives' as the sentient beings who are its very appearance and of whom it is the entire content of. Though he also experiences that as a human being he has the total free will to decide what he wants to do and to do it, he knows that whatever he thinks, wants, experiences, and does is exactly what he was supposed to as an appearance of that one Pure Consciousness that is his very content and whose appearance he is.

This being applicable just as much to others as to himself, the man of Advaita knows that he and they are being lived to perform their actions and are equally being lived to face the consequences of their actions, good or bad. As the understanding goes deeper and deeper within him, he will be lived more and more to accept the 'what is'. The 'what is' is the present, not the past, not the future, but the present that he lives in. He may use his intellect and free will to try to modify 'what is', but all the while he knows that whatever he is doing and whatever happens as a result is exactly what was supposed to happen. In any case, there is no question of resentment or resistance, just acceptance.

The man of Advaita has no anxiety about the results of his actions and can thus devote his attention and energy to the work at hand, without worrying about the results. He knows all the time that he and others are nothing but that Pure Consciousness that is their mutual content. He is thus totally free from the curse of judgment and feels one with others as fellow appearances of Consciousness in Consciousness.

Far from living life like a vegetable, or from being helpless with no personal will or intelligence, the man of Advaita lives the life of deep Understanding:

Life is an experience for the appearance that he is.

His Self image is of Consciousness, of and in which he is an appearance - as a human being.

THE PEACE OF THE SAGE

To a dealer in gold, it doesn't matter at all whether a gold ornament was skillfully or poorly crafted. His attention is on the gold that the ornament is composed of, not on what it looks like. His only interest is in the content of the ornament – the gold. It is only we who are concerned with the appearance of the ornament – whether it is beautiful or not.

Similarly to the Sage, it doesn't matter whether a thought is a so-called evil, hateful thought or a beautiful, loving thought, if at all he gets one. Because he is continuously aware that no matter what the thought may be it is just a movement in Consciousness, his attention rests entirely upon its content, on what the thought is composed of – Consciousness. It is only we who are concerned with what the thought is about, with its meaning or value.

In this way, the mind of the Sage remains spontaneously aware of God, or Consciousness, regardless of the outer appearance of things. Thus, the Sage always abides in perfect peace.

This is the supreme meditation of the Sage – the continuous awareness of the Indwelling Presence, i.e. Consciousness. While engaged with whatever he happens to be 'doing', he is always aware of his essential nature as Pure Consciousness.

NON-DOERSHIP

Life is nothing but 'doing'; either you are doing something or you are doing nothing, but you are 'doing' all the time.

Living is basically 'doing'.

If you believe that *you* are doing whatever it is that you are doing, then you thereby automatically separate yourself from the Source.

Whatever way you live then, you will always suffer from the pain of separation. No matter what you achieve or do not achieve, you will never be truly happy or content.

You will always want to achieve more and more, and never feel at peace. You will not know why, but the real reason is that you will be suffering from the pain of separation from the Source – from *your* Source.

On the other hand, if you are always conscious of the fact that it is not really *you* doing whatever it is that you appear to be doing, but the Source 'doing' it through you, then you thereby automatically stay connected with the Source, with God, with Consciousness, all the time.

This whole philosophy ultimately boils down to this one simple point: staying continually connected with the Source.

That is why Ramesh always emphasized this most direct approach to living Advaita: staying continually connected with the Source through the conscious awareness of 'non-doership'.

WHAT IS THE PURPOSE OF LIFE?

The purpose of life is living.
What is the purpose of living?
The purpose of living is experiencing.

There is nothing in life that is objectively good or bad, beautiful or ugly, desirable or undesirable... outside of the mind's imagination.

Life is experience.
Life is experiencing.

Life is either experiencing with judgment, or experiencing without judgment:
When there is judgment, life is turmoil.
When there is no judgment, life is Peace.

But, whether there is turmoil or Peace, life still continues to be nothing but experiencing.

I appear out of Consciousness, within Consciousness. I remain in Consciousness and experience life, and then I disappear once again back into Consciousness.

Meanwhile, life goes on…

And, Consciousness is all there is.

THE ACTOR AND THE ROLE

The actor can say "I am the role," but the role cannot say "I am the actor." The role is after all just an illusion.

How can an illusion say that it's real; how can a role say that it is the actor?

If an illusion claimed that it was real, that would only be part of the illusion.

If a role declared itself the actor, that would be part of its act as the role.

Just as an actor may experience himself as the illusory role that he plays, Consciousness can say "I AM xyz" as all of the egos.

But, if the egos are all illusions how can they say that

they are Consciousness…?

… Because, only Identified Consciousness in its role as an ego can 'realize' the Truth: Consciousness is all there is.

MANTRA OR JAPA

Mantra or repetition of the name of God is considered so important in Indian tradition because it keeps our attention grounded in the Divinity that WE ARE, causing our thoughts to go inward towards that Divinity rather than outward towards the distractions of the manifestation.

It is for this purpose that the traditional guru gives a Mantra to his disciple at the time of initiation.

The correct way to perform Japa, or Mantra, is with the Understanding that it is done solely for the remembrance of the Divinity within. There is to be no intention of *achieving* that Divinity in the misguided belief that it is something separate from That that we already are.

As Kabir says, "God is always with us."

According to Kabir all practices, including Japa, done with the belief that we are separate from God and that we can *achieve* God are worthless, as they only reinforce our sense of separation and doership.

True Japa is practiced in the firm belief that He is always with us, and that He and we are one.

Japa is thus done only with the intention of *remembering* Him and our oneness with Him.

By removing our feeling of separation and keeping us grounded in His Presence, Japa enables us to see the manifestation as nothing but His appearance even when our thoughts are being drawn outwards towards it.

Our life then becomes a prayer. This prayerful life is like a gold coin with duality on one side and Unicity on the other.

So long as the body is there, Identified Consciousness will also be there as Impersonal Consciousness identified with the body appearance.

Every thought in that Identified Consciousness will create

the ego with its sense of separation, or duality.

However, Japa performed with a proper understanding can help us to simultaneously be in touch with Unicity, so that both sides will appear equally on the gold coin of our life and living.

ADVAITIC GAYATRI

THE GAYATRI MANTRA

AUM BHUR BHUVA SWAHA
TAT SAVITUR VARENYAM
BHARGO DEVASYA DHEEMAHI
DHEEYOYONAHA PRACHODAYAT
AUM

The Gayatri Mantra occupies a pre-eminent position within the scriptures of Hinduism. From time immemorial our esteemed seers and saints have extolled the greatness of this mantra, and the importance of its daily recitation and meditation for our material and spiritual well being. In the Bhagavad Gita ch10:v36, Lord Krishna says, "In the Sama hymn of the Vedic hymns, I am known as Gayatri."

The usual Saguna (manifest) meaning of this mantra, as it is commonly understood is: "We meditate on the divine light of the sun. May it illumine our intellect." Though virtuous, this view remains external as it is concerned with the spiritual evolution of the ego. The Nirguna (unmanifest) meaning of the mantra orients us instead towards meditation on Existence-Consciousness-Bliss as the Supreme Self. However, the most profound method of performing the Gayatri Mantra is as a Supreme Yagnya* based upon Advaitic principles.

Each mantra has its own unique vibrations, which produce different effects depending upon the feelings and understanding with which it is uttered. The Gayatri Mantra is such a powerful mantra that it is generally considered to produce the highest vibrations of all of the mantras. It must thus have its beneficial effects no matter what meaning is given to it.

However, when performed with an Advaitic Understanding the Gayatri removes the clouds of ignorance, or Maya, that obscure the view of our true nature as Consciousness and cause us to become hypnotized by the drama of our apparent roles as human characters. This Maha Mantra now becomes a Maha Yagnya for the purpose of Self-Realization through the offering of 'that that we think we are', our egos, to the Divine Fire of the Pure Self that we truly are. This is the highest possible offering for any Yagnya.

Every time the Gayatri is chanted or meditated upon in this manner the Jivatma is being offered to the Paramatma, causing the Jivatma to increasingly realize that it and the Paramatma are one, that Identified Consciousness as the ego and Impersonal Consciousness are truly one.

*GAYATRI MANTRA AS A SUPREME YAGNA

A Yagnya is a ceremony that is performed for a profound spiritual purpose, wherein a divine sacrificial fire is ritually prepared into which one offers up that that one most values and covets. Therefore, to perform the Gayatri Yagnya, we must likewise precisely prepare the Yagnya's divine sacrifical fire, Impersonal Consciousness, by bringing it out until its glory shines forth from behind the veils of the three states of waking, dreaming, and deep sleep. We can only do this through sincere contemplation and meditation on our true nature. Anything less would be unworthy of the Gayatri Yagnya. Therefore, we inquire:

What is my true nature? Who or what am I?

I am not this body. I AM THAT that is aware of this body as a vehicle for its journey through life from birth to death.

I AM THAT that is aware of the acts that take place through this body according to its destiny. I AM THAT that is aware of this body when it is in the waking state, as the waking body. I AM THAT that is aware of this body when it is in the dreaming state, as the dream body. And, in the deep sleep state I AM THAT that still abides yet remains unaware of the body, or even of itself. There, there are no waves; the water is still. However, the body continues to live and breathe, and I continue to be, whether aware of the body or not.

I am not these emotions, feelings, and thoughts, which affect the body. I AM THAT in which they rise and set.

I am not this will and intellect. I AM THAT that is aware of them as they are being used in the acts that take place through the body.

I am not this personality, this individual, this ego. I AM THAT that is aware of the ego as it rises and sets with every thought.

I AM THAT that is aware of the ego's identification with this body and of the changing modifications to that identification such as, "I am thin," "I am fat," "I am strong," "I am weak," etc.

I AM THAT that is aware of how the ego claims ownership of the acts that take place through the body according to its destiny.

I AM THAT that is aware of the ego as it identifies with an occupation or a position in life, e.g. a doctor, a lawyer, a driver, a clerk, etc.

I AM THAT that is aware of the ego as it identifies with perceived good or bad qualities within itself, e.g. "I am loving," "I am kind," "I am arrogant," or "I am selfish."

I AM THAT that is aware of the ego as it identifies with certain relationships in life, e.g. "I am a husband," "I am a father," "I am a friend," etc.

I AM THAT that is aware of the ego as it identifies with the so called achievements or failures that take place according to the body's destiny.

I AM THAT that is aware of the ego as it identifies with various emotions, feelings, or thoughts, e.g. "I am angry," "I am hurt," "I am thoughtful," etc.

I AM THAT that is aware of the ego as it identifies

with its free will and intellect, e.g. "I am strong willed," "I am intelligent," "I can do it!" etc.

I AM THAT that is aware of the ego as it identifies itself with a name, e.g. "I am Chaitanya Balsekar."

I AM THAT that is aware of the ego as it identifies with certain assets or possessions and thinks, "I am rich" or "I am poor."

Who or what am I then? Who or what am I who is aware of all these things, yet remains independent of them? Who or what am I in my own right?

I...AM. I EXIST. I am Existence, Pure Impersonal Consciousness, the Impersonal Presence in which all of these things rise and set as thoughts.

I do not have to think or believe that I exist; I KNOW I exist. That KNOWLEDGE, prior to thought, I AM. If I lose my memory, though I may go around asking who I am, I will not question whether I exist or not. I KNOW I exist. But, the moment I think or say "I AM," I have moved out of KNOWLEDGE into thought, into the ego.

That Impersonal Consciousness that is aware of this body as Identified Consciousness, I AM. That that is aware as thought of the actions that take place through this body, I AM.

That Impersonal Consciousness that is aware as Identified Consciousness of the emotions, feelings, and thoughts acting upon this body, I AM. That Impersonal Consciousness that is aware as Identified Consciousness of having free will and intellect, I AM.

That Impersonal Consciousness that as Identified Consciousness is aware of all of the various activities of the ego as thoughts, I AM.

I do not have to think "I AM." I do not have to believe "I AM." I know I AM, prior to thought.

Impersonal Consciousness is Unicity. Identified Consciousness is duality. Thought only arises within Identified Consciousness, thus creating the identification with the body known as the ego.

The question then arises: How did Impersonal Consciousness – so vast, infinite, and eternal – ever become limited by the body and the ego?

Within the manifestation, which is composed entirely of Consciousness, when a body is born or makes its appearance Impersonal Consciousness gets reflected in that body as Identified Consciousness, I AM, and appears as such from the body's birth until its death. The reflected I AM, or Identified Consciousness, gets identified with that body and a body/mind unit gets created. All of the thoughts that arise within this identified I AM get associated thereby with that body/mind unit.

Every thought has its two ends, like the two ends of a stick: the subject end and the object end. The subject end is always the ego that is associated with the body, while the object end will be whatever it may be in each particular case. Thus, every thought re-creates the ego identified with that particular body, and that ego continuously rises and sets again with each new thought. Therefore, Identified Consciousness is actually the essence of the ego. The ego is basically one of the countless roles that Consciousness is playing in the drama of life. By the power of Maya (Divine Hypnosis), the illusory role begins to think that it is real, and the true Actor (Consciousness) is pushed into the background behind the body/mind's three states of waking, dreaming, and deep sleep.

Through this contemplation, we have now come to the Understanding of our true nature, of what we really are: the all pervading Impersonal Consciousness or Pure Awareness.

The coverings of the body/mind's three states of waking, dreaming, and deep sleep have now been removed and the I AM, that Pure Existence-Consciousness-Awareness, has been brought out in all its pristine glory.

This is the Divine Sacrificial Fire of the Gayatri Yagnya, into which the illusory ego is being lived to offer itself when the Gayatri Mantra is recited with an Advaitic Understanding.

In the Katha Upanishad Nachiketa reprimands his father, insisting that he must offer that that he most cherishes to the Divine Fire in order for the Yagnya to be sincere. In a burst of irritation, the father says that he will offer Nachiketa himself since he is that that is most near and dear to him. In the same way, for this Gayatri Yagnya, what could possibly be nearer and dearer to the ego than the ego itself? When the ego is being lived to sacrifice itself to the burning fire of Truth, the Gayatri Mantra becomes that highest possible Yagnya that will inevitably move Yama, the god of death, to fully reveal the Understanding and Knowledge of our true nature.

Performing The Gayatri Yagnya

As stated earlier, the usual meaning given to the Gayatri is: "We meditate on the divine light of the sun; may it illumine our intellect."

However, our interpretation on the basis of Advaita is as follows:

Aum Bhur Bhuva Swaha:
Aum: A OH OO MM.
A: waking state, OH: dreaming state, OO: deep sleep state, MMMMM: I AM.

Aum: I AM beyond the three body states of waking, dreaming, and deep sleep.

Bhur Bhuva Swaha: beyond the body, mind, and intellect.

Tat Savitu Varenyam: that divinity worthy of veneration.

Bhargo Devasya Dheemahi: the ego, divinely purified, is being lived to offer itself.

Dheeyoyonaha Prachodayata: knowledge manifests to realize – That that You are, I AM.

We must first become aware of the I AM, the Divine Sacrificial Fire of the Yagnya, through Contemplation and Meditation.

Then the ego – that that is most dear and precious to us – is repeatedly offered to this Divine Presence to realize its oneness with and subservience to it, to be burnt in the fire of purification and clarity until it can no longer bind us, until it becomes completely worthless like burnt ash.

AUM BHUR BHUVA SWAHA
TAT SAVITU VARENYAM
BHARGO DEVASYA DHEEMAHI
DHEEYOYONAHA PRACHODAYATA
AUM

"To the I AM, beyond the three states of waking, dreaming, and deep sleep,

Beyond the body, mind, and intellect,

That Divinity worthy of veneration,

This ego, divinely purified, offers itself,

And Knowledge manifests to realize that there are not two."

"To that Life that is the substratum of the three states of the body, this ego – which is also a manifestation of that same Life – offers itself, and Understanding arises that You are there as I AM."

The mechanism of the ego continues to function so long as the life in the body causes thoughts to rise and set within Identified Consciousness, but it now awakens to its illusory nature, and loses the sense of doership that had previously been the source of so much imaginary confusion and suffering. Now, the ego understands that it does not live but is being lived as a role played by Consciousness in the drama of life. This 'awakened' ego becomes like a burnt rope that, though still visible, can no longer bind – such a rope is useless, a mere appearance, there but not there – until just the shadow of 'a person' *remains*.

As one goes on reciting the Gayatri Mantra with this Understanding, one's attention gets increasingly directed towards the Impersonal Presence that shines forth from behind the veil of appearances, the Impersonal Consciousness that one truly is, and less and less towards the ego that one previously thought one was. One's Self Image becomes that of Pure Awareness, and not that of a separate 'individual'. There is a quantum leap from belief to Knowledge prior to thought. **

**Acknowledgement: I am deeply grateful to the late Dr. T.K.N. Trivikram Ph.D, and his remarkable book 'Divine Yoga of the Soul' (self-published: 52 Shivaji Park, Mumbai 400028), for inspiring me to give this Advaitic interpretation of the Gayatri Mantra. Though his book is mainly concerned with Sri Vidya and Kundalini, his interpretation of the vital words in the Gayatri was most helpful and enlivening. Dr. Trivikram studied Sanskrit very deeply and it was his contention that we should give that meaning to the mantras that they had when they were first uttered during Vedic times. The original meaning of a word might be quite different from the current dictionary meaning, which is based upon the passage of time. In the Gayatri, 'Bhargo' is normally given the dictionary meaning of 'light', but Dr. Trivikram found out that it originally meant 'something that was purified through repeated burnings in fire'. Therefore, 'Bhargo' can also be taken to mean an ego which has been purified through repeated firings of Sadhana, so that it is now qualified to perform the Gayatri Yagna. Another very important word is 'Dheemahi'; its usual dictionary meaning is 'meditate', however Dr. Trivikram has interpreted it as 'offer'. 'Dheeyoyonaha Prachodayata' is normally taken to mean 'May it illumine our intellect', but Dr. Trivikram translated it as 'Knowledge manifests to realize — That that You are, I AM.*

A DAILY THANKSGIVING TO ONE'S PERSONAL DEITY

You are Impersonal Awareness, Consciousness, Bliss – All Pervading, All Powerful, and All Knowing – One without a second. In You, we live and move and have our being.

In all our love for You, we have given You a name and form, since it is easier to love and worship the Personal rather than the Impersonal.

You are our beloved "Shri MANGESH," a form of SHIVA. This is our name for You, our family deity. Others will give You their own name, as they wish.

You dwell inside of us. You protect us. You multiply our allotment of good.

Thank You Shri MANGESH for the great bounty you bestow upon us, and thank You for multiplying it day by day in so many perfect ways.

In all of Your love for us Shri MANGESH, You have given us the Understanding of our true nature – that we are nothing but roles played by You, the Divine Actor, in the Divine Movie of this manifestation.

In this Divine Movie, You alone are the Actor, the Writer, the Director, and the Producer, as well as the entire audience.

Whatever I experience of myself or of this manifestation arises entirely in the world of thought: vibrations rising and setting within You. You are the sole content of thought, and as such, You are all there is.

Whenever I 'think', or rather, whenever a thought arises within the Consciousness I AM, as reflected in this human body, 'my' ego arises together with the thought.

As You are the sole content of *all* thought, You are therefore also the sole content of 'me', the ego. You are all there is.

May I always be consciously aware of myself as being nothing but You appearing in the form of this body and ego.

You are all there is.

May I always be consciously aware that the other people, beings, and objects in this world, are really You appearing as them. You are all there is.

May I always be consciously aware that this entire manifestation is really only You appearing as this manifestation. You are all there is.

Just as it is always water, whether appearing as rivers, waves, or oceans, You always remain MANGESH, or Consciousness, whether appearing as egos, beings, or objects. You are all there is.

How could I ever be separate from You, MANGESH? How could I ever be alone?

As long as I am here, as a part of this manifestation, You will always be here with me, as me, and as this manifestation. You are all there is.

Whatever I may think, or feel, or do by the use of my intellect and free will, is truly nothing but You acting in this role, as this ego. You are all there is.

Whatever 'others', as parts of this manifestation, may think, or feel, or do by the use of their intellect and free will, is truly nothing other than You acting in the roles of those egos. You are all there is. Let me be lived to always be consciously aware of this Truth.

Shri MANGESH, so long as I am here in this form, let me be lived to love and worship You with all of my heart, knowing that You and I are 'not-two'. You are all there is, Shri MANGESH; You are all there is. Thank You for this Divine Understanding, which You have graciously bestowed upon me. Thank You, Thank You, Thank You.

THERE IS NO PARTING

As one grows older, one misses so many people who are now no more: loved ones, near and dear ones, good friends, acquaintances, and even just people one has only read or heard about... all those who are now no more.

Some may be missed terribly or even painfully, their absence deeply regretted.

In some cases, it can even seem unbearable for those who remain behind to continue on alone...

However, with the Understanding of Advaita, we no longer grieve for the dead because we know that they were all mere appearances – they were all just appearances of Consciousness on the screen of Consciousness itself.

Having been composed entirely of Consciousness

from the very beginning, they have now returned to their Source – they have become one with Consciousness again.

Therefore, we need not grieve for them.

We may still miss them from time to time, but in truth we actually feel happy for them to be relieved of the burden of duality.

We do not grieve for them because we know that there can be no parting.

After all, who were all those people who are now no more? They were all manifestations of the 'one life' that animates all of the different bodies on whom we then project illusory personalities, or egos.

Now that same life has ceased to animate those particular body appearances, so we say that they have 'died'.

Though we may still miss those appearances when the memory of them arises in the form of a thought, we know that WE ARE that same 'one life'.

That that was previously animating them is That that is

now animating us.

There is no parting.
There never was any parting.

We are all that 'one life' that is beyond birth and death, unborn and undying...

Meanwhile, as human beings, we are all dreamed characters in this manifestation that is the *Dream of Consciousness*.

The author may be contacted by email:
chaitaneela1@rediffmail.com

For further details, contact:
Yogi Impressions Books Pvt. Ltd.
1711, Centre 1, World Trade Centre,
Cuffe Parade, Mumbai 400 005, India.

Fill in the Mailing List form on our website
and receive, via email, information on
books, authors, events and more.
Visit: www.yogiimpressions.com

Telephone: (022) 22155036/7/8
Fax: (022) 22155039
E-mail: yogi@yogiimpressions.com

 Join us on Facebook:
www.facebook.com/yogiimpressions

 Follow us on Twitter:
www.twitter.com/yogiimpressions

ALSO PUBLISHED BY YOGI IMPRESSIONS

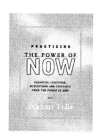

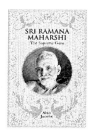

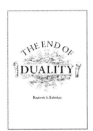

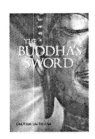

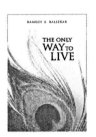

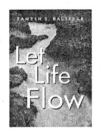

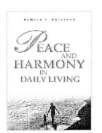

   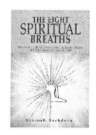

DVDs

AUDIO CDs

Create greater balance and wholeness within yourself with

synchronicity®
Contemporary High-Tech Meditation® Audio CDs

When meditation was first conceived thousands of years ago, its techniques were suited for a simple, very different way of life. Today, we live in a chaotic, high-stress environment where time, calm and clarity can be elusive.

The Synchronicity Experience: quite simply, it meditates you
Its proprietary Holodynamic® Vibrational Entrainment Technology (HVET) developed by its Founder, Master Charles Cannon, is embedded in musical meditation soundtracks that literally meditate you while you listen.

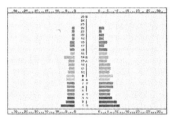
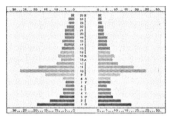

Brain monitor of a typical non-meditator shows pronounced hemispheric imbalance and fragmented, limited brain function.

A regular user of Synchronicity Contemporary High-Tech Meditation® develops a high degree of synchronization indicating whole brain function.

Taking the guesswork and randomness out of the meditative process, the meditation soundtracks are available in the Alpha and Theta formats for light and medium meditation. Whether you are an experienced meditator or just starting to meditate, our CDs will help deliver a four-fold increase in results compared to traditional methods.

Om

Om Namah Shivaya

Harmonic Coherence

Welcome To My World

Om Mani Padme Hum

Sounds Of Source
Vol. 1-5

Time Off

Song Of The Ecstatic

Romancing The
Moment
The Love Meditation

For more details, visit: www.yogiimpressions.com